PART-TIME
FATHER

PART-TIME FATHER

Edith Atkin & Estelle Rubin

The Vanguard Press, Inc. New York

PUBLISHED SIMULTANEOUSLY IN CANADA BY GAGE PUBLISHING CO., AGINCOURT, ONTARIO.

LIBRARY OF CONGRESS CATALOGUE CARD NUMBER: 75-18428

ISBN: 0-8149-0766-0

DESIGNER: ELIZABETH WOLL

MANUFACTURED IN THE UNITED STATES OF AMERICA.

ACKNOWLEDGMENTS

To acknowledge here all the persons who helped us write this book would be impossible. Our special thanks must go first to our patients—the fathers, mothers, and children of divorce who made us aware of that neglected man: the part-time father and his full-time problems.

There are, in addition, the many persons whose help we enlisted and who cooperated willingly and generously with us in our undertaking:

The fathers, mothers, children, grandparents, colleagues, friends, relatives, who had gone through the anguish of the breakup of their families and who submitted themselves to our inquiries, despite the pain it may have caused them.

Our professional colleagues whom we consulted when we ran into a snag or disagreed between ourselves on some theoretical issue. Among them we wish to thank especially Samuel Atkin, M.D., Charles Feigelson, M.D., Robert Popkin, M.D., Herman Roiphe, M.D., and Robert Sayer, M.D., who also shared with us their experience with divorced patients.

We would like to single out for special thanks Peter Neubauer, M.D., Director of the Child Development Center, Jewish Board of Guardians, New York, who encouraged us throughout this project and gave us unstintingly of his time and counsel.

Leonard Karlin of Chicago, Nancy Wechsler and Shirley Fingerhood of New York City, attorneys who educated us in the legal aspects of separation and divorce.

Phyllis Rubenton, librarian at The New York Psychoanalytic Institute, who kept us supplied with literature on divorce and who tracked down for us any book or article we expressed interest in, no matter how vague the request.

Our publishers, the Vanguard Press: Dana Randt, who raised so many astute questions; Miriam Shrifte, who made invaluable suggestions; and Bernice Woll, who has been called—and, indeed, is—"the ideal editor." We cannot be too grateful for her perceptive intelligence, and her grace and clarity of expression that have so enriched us.

Helen Atkin and Mary Stefanich, who miraculously deciphered our handwriting and typed the manuscript, sometimes far into the night.

Last but certainly not least, our husbands, Samuel Atkin and Jonathan Rubin, who gave so freely of their moral support during the many months of our labor.

To them and to our many friends who cheered us on, we offer our deepest thanks.

THE AUTHORS

"There's a blessing on the hearth,
a special providence for fatherhood."

Robert Browning
in *The Ring and the Book*

CONTENTS

INTRODUCTION

This is a book about the separated or divorced father and his relationship to his children. It is also, tangentially, about the separated or divorced mother, since, though she is physically removed, her invisible presence hovers over that relationship.

In our work with children of separation and divorce—children from all social strata—we were struck by the plight of the father in his part-time role. Since mothers are given custody of the children in some 85 to 90 percent of divorces, fathers are turned into visiting or part-time parents—an unnatural, ill-fitting, uncomfortable situation at best, at least at the beginning. The fathers we saw wanted very much to do what was best for their children but were in a quandary. How to go about it in their changed role? Some who failed as fathers did so from omission rather than commission; from ignorance rather than callousness; from unintentional neglect rather than lack of love. They all wanted—sometimes desperately—to be good fathers. And some sought help to do so.

They came with problems ranging from mundane matters, such as what to do with the children on visiting day and whether it was all right to have their girl friends along, to deep concern about their emotional relationships with the children, especially about their children's negative reactions—anger, hostility, accusations, depression, silence—and, even more painful, about their own reactions, whether in response to the children's negative feelings or to evidence, real or fancied, of their ex-wife's influence on the youngsters.

These fathers were often disheartened, feeling they had little place or value in their children's lives and some were tempted to give up from discouragement or feelings of rejection by their children. Many of their frustrations and disappointments, we found, arose from their using old yardsticks for a new life style. They were saddened by the obligatory, overt changes in their function as fathers, confusing such changes with a fundamental alteration in the nature of their relationship to the children.

The observations gleaned in the course of our work as therapists over many years prompted us to write this book. It deals with the variety of problems a divorced father faces with his children at different stages of their development, from infancy through adolescence, and also at different stages of the divorce, from the breakup of the family to the evolving relationship of father and child as time goes on and both adjust to the divorce situation. It also tries to deal not only with the problems of the separated or divorced father but with his potentialities and opportunities for a fulfilling and gratifying relationship with his children.

We hope this book will give men and women—especially fathers—struggling with the problems of separation and divorce a better understanding of themselves and their children and help them come to terms with the altered functions created by their changed family situation. Most of all, we hope this book will give our readers a better understanding of the importance of fathering in the lives of children and will instill in separated or divorced fathers a better appreciation of how much they mean to their children—and how much their children mean to them.

Part I

UPROOTINGS AND UPHEAVALS

1
IN LIMBO

Because they are divorced, millions of men must live apart from their children and must make special arrangements to see them. True, there are family men who seldom see their children because of their work or other circumstances. But their relationship is of a quite different nature from that of the man who is no longer a part of the family and whose time with his children is decreed by law. It is with the latter, the part-time fathers—and their relationship with their children that this book is concerned.

Ten years ago one out of six marriages ended in divorce. Today the figure is two out of five. And the rate, statisticians tell us, is rising. The escalating divorce rate is forcing us to take a new look at the divorced family; to see it not as an occasional deviation from the traditional family structure as Western civilization has known it for centuries, but as a new life style.

Divorce involving children—and most divorces do involve children—has created new family patterns for which as yet we have no guidelines. Other significant events in our lives have their prescribed rites. Births, confirmations, commencement exercises, wedding ceremonies, funeral services—all these mark special social occasions to which we respond with conventional social forms. We bring gifts, extend good wishes, offer congratulations or condolences. For the momentous event of the death of a marriage there are no ceremonies (except perhaps a consoling or congratulatory drink with friends) to ease the former partners' adjustment to their changing status; no rituals on which to rely in their groping toward a new life.

Conflicting Advice

Following the breakup of the marriage, the divorced father is confronted with countless situations for which he has no preparation. No longer a husband but still a father, he finds himself with a large part of his life "exed" out—ex-husband, ex-son-in-law, ex-brother-in-law, ex-uncle—with no cultural supports to meet the altered relationships.

All the divorced father finds is a plethora of conflicting advice. For instance, some psychologists advise that there be no contact between the divorced parents. Such eminent authorities as Joseph Goldstein, Anna Freud, and Albert J. Solnit, in their *Beyond the Best Interests of the Child,* go so far as to state that the noncustodial parent (usually the father) "should have no legally enforceable right to visit the child and the custodial parent should have the right to decide whether it is desirable for the child to have such visits." On the other hand, some authorities advise the noncustodial parent to remain in close touch with the child and the divorced parents to remain friendly for the sake of the child. Such conflicting opinions only compound the divorced father's confusion about his role as father and ex-spouse.

The Plight of the Part-Time Father

Very little has been written about the plight of the separated or divorced father. Given the traditional roles of man and woman in our culture, it is generally assumed that the man is responsible for the breakup of the family. Since he is nearly always the one to leave the home—*whether he wants to or not*—he is regarded as the obvious culprit. The facts are, however, that not infrequently—and increasingly so—it is the wife who wants "out," who wants to free herself from what she feels is an intolerable or life-crushing marital situation. Nonetheless, the stereotype persists of the divorced man as a self-centered, pleasure-seeking male who has walked out on his devoted wife and loving children, usually, if not always, for "another woman." For many, if not most separated or divorced fathers, nothing could be further from the truth.

The plight of the separated or divorced mother, on the other hand, has received much public attention. And with good reason. On her own, without assistance, she can find the task of raising children burdensome. More often than not, she must work to make ends meet, and this means she must arrange for the children's care, which may be fitful or inadequate. And throughout, she is restricted not only by her children but also by the limited social opportunities now open to her. Most separated or divorced mothers, let's face it, have a very hard time of it.

The mother's difficulties, however, in no way minimize the father's. Though of a different order from hers, his problems are no less great. In some ways, particularly in regard to his relationship with his children, they may be even greater.

Loneliness

There are, of course, the immediate social problems that the newly divorced or separated man must cope with. Loneliness and the disruption of old habits and routines are among the toughest experiences he must face after the breakup of the family. Few men are prepared for these miseries.

"The worst thing of all was the loneliness," Jack L., thirty-eight, confided about his separation from his family after twelve years of marriage. "The loneliness and the discombobulation of your whole way of life. At the beginning I was so lonely, especially for the kids, I felt like asking Elsie to take me back. I'd hate to tell you how many times I picked up the phone to call her. Thank God I had sense enough to hang up before she answered. We'd split and gone back together a dozen times. It never worked out and I knew it would be crazy to try again. This time I knew I just had to stick it out. Sometimes I'd feel so sorry for myself I'd cry.

"You can't imagine how dreary it is, living by yourself in a hotel room—and a third-rate hotel at that—after twelve years of family life. And having to watch every penny I spent, since half my salary went to Elsie and the children. It meant going without a new suit, even thinking twice about going to a movie. Taking all my meals in cheap restaurants. I'd get so sick of restaurant food day after day that sometimes I'd just buy myself a sandwich and bring it up to the room to eat while I watched the boob tube. I felt so low that even when old friends asked me over, I'd sometimes turn down the invitation. I thought they were inviting me because they felt sorry for me or wanted to tell me something nasty Elsie had said about me.

"Well, after a while you make the best of it—though you never really get used to it. You get to talking with people, you find other guys in the same spot. You go out together, have a few beers, maybe meet some girls. . . . But it sure is hell in the beginning."

Seeing the Children—By Appointment Only

His own physical and social readjustments are minor compared to the artificial arrangements a separated or divorced father often must make to see his children. Now to be with them he must abide by legal stipulations known as visitation rights. As one father lamented, "I have to make an appointment to see my own children." He must arrange to meet them at an appointed hour and a designated place for a specific length of time. If the child is very young, the meeting between father and child usually takes place in the home of the mother, often a queasy situation at best. One young father described his visits with his ten-month-old son: "Helen is good about going out when I come to visit with Roddy. But her mother is always around, giving me dirty looks. If Roddy puts the toy I brought him in his mouth, there she is, Johnny-on-the-spot, complaining that he'll get sick from the germs on it. Much as I love to play with him, sometimes I can hardly wait to get out of there because of her."

Some mothers, either for personal reasons or because the father is unreliable about the time he picks the children up or brings them back, will press their right as custodial parent to set precise limits for visiting, as stipulated in the separation or divorce agreement. Many fathers find such rigidity especially hard to take. Jim B. complains, "My work takes me away from the city for long periods of time, and sometimes I don't see Billy [age five] for a month, though I try to call him once a week. The other night when I got into town I thought I'd surprise him with a teddy bear I bought at the airport. When I got to the door, there was Judy, looking at me as though I was Frankenstein. She wouldn't let me in because Billy was asleep, she said. Maybe she had some guy in there and she didn't want me to know. Not that I give a damn. She wouldn't even take the teddy bear for Billy because then he'd know I'd been there and didn't see him and he'd be upset. As a concession she said she'd permit me to see Bill the next day, even though my time with him was Saturdays. Imagine! 'permit' me to see my own child!"

In the new situation the separated or divorced father isn't quite certain how to behave with his children. As one newly divorced father explained, "You feel you can't just 'be' with your kids. You must 'do things' with them, entertain them, see that they have a good time." Another father said, "I'm more like a good-time Charlie than a father."

Another torment the part-time father suffers is the thought of leaving the children to the mercies of a woman whom the acid of divorce has stripped of human form and revealed as a man-eating piranha. He is afraid she will poison their minds, turn them against him. Equally painful is the fear that as a part-time father he has lost the opportunity to shape their values or influence their development. He is afraid that now he can only participate in the periphery of their lives. When he is lonely and sad, he sometimes wonders if the separation from the children was too big a price to pay for reprieve from a slow death.

Inner Turmoil

No one, no matter how emotionally stable, can go through the ordeal of a divorce—and all the wretchedness that precedes it—without being emotionally affected by it. Even the solacing arms of another woman give no immunity against the emotional upheavals that follow in the wake of a divorce. You find yourself depressed, self-pitying, full of anger and resentment one moment, guilt-ridden and self-castigating the next. Your world has come apart at the seams. You feel uprooted, uncertain of your course. As one father put it when asked how he felt after he obtained his divorce, "Man, you're nowhere."

Divorce, with or without children, is always a painful business. In our society, where marriage, and certainly young marriage, is usually the fruition of romantic love, divorce marks the crushing of youthful dreams, the mockery of vows ("I pledge my troth"), the repudiation of former love, and, not infrequently, the breeding of bitterness and hate. Even when the divorce has been longed for, fought for, or connived at, there is something about the severance of marital ties, no matter how onerous they may have been or how courageous the act, that carries with it a sense of failure, of self-diminishment.

Although the temporary reaction may be one of enormous relief, especially if the process has been tarred with acrimony and vindictiveness, when children are involved there almost inevitably follow feelings of guilt, of doubt, of uncertainty. Even though, in the long run, divorce may be the saving grace for children of an irreparable union, those children often pay an immediate price in unhappiness and, quite possibly, in emotional or behavioral disturbances. Their distress is a painful reminder to the father of his blighted hopes.

A father's longing for his children, his loss of family, home, friends, are all too often overlooked. Indeed, one can imagine a touch of envy in the fantasies of his fettered male friends: "Single again! Now he can play the field." But playing the field holds little attraction, at least early in the separation or divorce. "A lot of newly divorced men," says divorce lawyer Robert V. Sherwin in the *Wall Street Journal*, "want sex about as much as a man getting over dysentery wants a big meal."

Divorce—the Tie That Binds

Cutting the bonds of matrimony in no way means cutting the emotional bonds that weld together a man and woman, especially if they have once been in love. Mixed-up feelings of love, hate, guilt, anger, resentment, spite, and jealousy can hold a divorced couple in bondage to each other for years. Sometimes for life. Ironically, for some ex-partners those very hang-ups that made it impossible for them to live together amicably may be the forces that keep them tied to each other.

The emotional shackles of divorce are generally so well disguised that both parties may be quite unaware of them. They may take the form, for example, of frequent telephone calls or letters, ostensibly about the children's welfare, or of never-ending legal battles claiming violations of the contract regarding support or visitation rights. Or they may take the guise of "let's-be-civilized-about-this," with Daddy coming to dinner once a week, supposedly for the sake of the children but really to keep tabs on the ex-partner.

Severing the ties when you share responsibility for offspring is no easy task. If your child is an infant and the visits to the baby take place in your former home, even though your ex-wife discreetly absents herself, constant reminders of your life together—the lamp you bought in the flea market, your wife's first painting on the wall, the lounge chair you used to sit in, the wallpaper you never liked in the bathroom, the marriage bed—all keep your feelings stirred up and hinder the process of letting go.

Genuine concern for the children can provide a legitimate cover for continuing to hang on to the old relationship. Mother calls in a distressed voice: "Susie's been running a fever three nights in a row. What should I do?" A sensible reply would be, "Call a doctor." But Father seizes on the illness not only as an excuse to come over and comfort his sick child but also to see what's going on with his ex-wife. Or Mother calls to say that Susie is running a fever and can't go out with her father today. But he can, of course, visit with her at home. Father comes over, Mother serves him a drink. Susie is delighted that she has both parents around her. Maybe they'll get back together again! Farfetched as it may seem, we have known children who are always getting sick not only as a means of possibly bringing Daddy back, but also as an unconscious compliance with the needs of the ex-partners to keep the attachment going.

Some divorced parents pride themselves on the friendly relationship they have arrived at once the battles have subsided. Amy reports, "Bert and I get along much better since we've been divorced than we ever did when we were married. He comes over every Saturday to do the heavy chores around the house—he cuts the grass, paints the kitchen, repairs the furniture. He never used to lift a finger to help me before. And he uses the washing machine for his laundry. That's a laugh. Before, he wouldn't dream of washing so much as a pair of socks. It's nice for the kids having him around the house. The trouble is, they keep asking me why Daddy can't come back and stay here with us."

It can be a comfort to children to see that their parents no longer regard each other as monsters. But there is also the risk that the casual presence of the divorced father in the home will nourish the child's fantasy—especially the young child's—that the parents will be reunited. To avoid this risk, and to help children adjust to the realities of their changed family situation, meetings between the ex-spouses should be avoided as far as possible. Some authorities go so far as to advocate no contact whatever between the divorced parents except through intermediaries. We respect the mental health principles inherent in this viewpoint. But it is unrealistic. Although you are no longer a husband, you share parenthood with your former spouse as long as you live. Occasions arise when contact between the two of you is inevitable. A child is in a serious accident or is ill. Or he must change schools. Or he runs away, or gets arrested, or needs psychiatric help, or graduates from high school, or gets married.

It is not so much the actual contact between the parents as the unconscious clinging to the old relationship—be it in the guise of everlasting fights, complaints to friends and relatives, or, most painful to children, efforts to pry out of them what goes on in the household of the other—that bespeaks a divorce in name only.

Achieving a divorce in fact as well as in name is a slow, painful, resistant process. It may take a long time—sometimes years—especially if you are embroiled in recurrent dealings with your ex-wife over the children. Or over money. (In many divorces the two are interchangeable objects of barter.) As a divorced man you are no longer legally married, but neither are you single. At least not until you have recovered your bearing as an independent, self-respecting person, free of the sticky bonds of an unhappy marriage. Time and the exigencies of life generally bring this about eventually. But only if you guard against the emotional pulls backward that keep you wallowing in self-pity or regret. Only if you work at it, force yourself if necessary to step forward into a new life. Only when you have finally shed the skin of your old marriage will you emerge as a free, whole person, your own man. Only then will you be single again.

Divorce as Cataclysm for Children

As for the children, after the divorce all hell seems to break loose. Suddenly every child "acts up." The baby is banging his head against the crib. The three-year-old has nightmares and is afraid of the dark. Five-year-old Johnny starts wetting the bed. Jimmy, eleven, complains of headaches each morning and wants to stay home from school. Twelve-year-old Sally is already running around with boys. Mary, fifteen, fights with everyone in the house and cries if you say Boo to her. Joe, sixteen, takes dope and threatens to leave home. Eighteen-year-old Katie actually does leave home. She drops out of college and goes off to live with her boy friend in a commune.

Mother, the custodial parent, is beside herself with worry. She feels helpless and overwhelmed in the face of these problems. Father, who has abdicated his place as authority figure in the home, feels equally helpless and overwhelmed. The parents flagellate themselves with guilt and self-doubt. At the same time, each secretly blames the other for their children's troubles.

Of course children react, sometimes violently, to the earthquake in their lives. How could they not be disturbed by the disruption of their family? Indeed, if a child showed no reaction, it would be cause for worry. Father has left home. When he comes to see them, Mother and he quarrel over when he is supposed to pick them up and bring them back. Mother complains about money. She cries a lot. She used to be home when the children came from school, and gave them snacks. Now she works, and when she gets back at night, she's tired and cranky. Father comes on Saturday and takes them to lunch. Then he brings them home and goes away, and they don't see him again until next Saturday.

No matter how well prepared children have been for the breakup, when it finally happens it leaves them frightened, shaken. All children feel abandoned when their father moves out, even when they know it is against his wishes. "What will happen to me now?" they wonder. "If Father left, maybe Mother will leave too. Who will take care of me?" The thought terrifies. No wonder that, under such terror, small children break out with physical symptoms and behavior problems.

Sowing Dragons' Teeth

Although it appears that children "suddenly" act up after the divorce, we know that the seeds of their troubles were sown earlier, in a "dry season." Children are sensitive barometers of the atmosphere at home. Despite the disclaimers of some men and women—"I was thunderstruck when he (she) asked me for a divorce. I always thought we were so happy together. So did our friends"—a separation or divorce seldom happens out of the blue. It is usually the burst boil of marital unhappiness that has been festering, sometimes for years.

Preoccupied with their own miseries, parents may overlook or minimize a child's signals of distress during the trying times before the actual break. Once the separation occurs, the child's disturbed behavior becomes starkly visible, especially when it involves school or community. No wonder he steals, or goes on drugs, or runs away, announce the amateur pundits. He comes from a broken home! In these days, when the blame for children's problems is all too readily attributed to parental sins, the child's troubles are pointed at with righteous indignation by the aggrieved parent and viewed with painful guilt by the aggrieving one. The neighbors point an accusing finger at both. Yet if one had dared to look before the separation took place, dark portents of trouble ahead could already have been seen, as anyone working with emotionally disturbed children knows full well.

Have We Harmed the Children?

Have we harmed the children by the divorce? anguished parents ask themselves. Have we made them pay for the resolution of our unhappiness? Should we have stuck it out for their sake or at least waited until they were grown? There is hardly a divorced parent, sick at heart over a child's misery, who hasn't at some time or other asked himself these questions.

What can one say? Certainly divorce is bad for children. Of course it would be better for your children to be brought up in a home with two parents who love and care about each other, who give physical and emotional sustenance to each other, so that they are able in turn to give their children the love and emotional nourishment they need for healthy development. But parents whose marriage has disintegrated beyond the point of no return do not have this option. They must make a decision, to save themselves whatever the cost or to try to stick it out. One does what one must. There are parents who "sacrifice" themselves for the sake of keeping a home intact for the children. (Often, motives less virtuous than self-sacrifice enter into their staying together, such as fear of other people's opinion, dread of the unknown, feelings of failure, neurotic ties, and in some instances, religious convictions.) If you know these parents well, you may find that they derive satisfaction, perverse though it may be, from their martyrdom or even from their tormenting of each other. But the children of these unhappy unions pay a price, though in a different way, for chronic exposure to a poisoned atmosphere.

Perhaps the better question to ask is not, Have the children been harmed by the divorce? but rather, Would they have been more harmed if we had stayed together after our marriage went bad? Who is to say that the scars are deeper from divorce than from constant exposure to parental conflict and hate?

There can be no ready answers. Each child reacts to the separation of his parents in his own way, depending upon age, emotional maturity, stage of development, health, relationship to each parent, place in the family, and countless other complicated factors that we don't know how to reckon with. In the same family one child is devastated by the breakup; another seems to weather it calmly.

Some things we do know. We know, for example, that for some children deliverance from the parental war, whether hot or cold, is an enormous relief: We have known children unable to function due to tension over their parents' fighting, children plagued with minor illnesses or failing in school. Relieved of the conflict, their health improved, they were able to put their minds to their schoolwork, they relaxed in the wake of the peace and quiet that followed a separation.

For whatever comfort it may afford, studies have shown that children of divorce have fewer problems than children living in two-parent homes where marital discord is rampant.

Dr. Louise Despert, in *Children of Divorce*, found that among the children she treated for emotional disturbance, there were far fewer children of divorce than there were proportionately among the general population, which includes both well-adjusted children and children in difficulties. "Divorce is not automatically destructive to children; the marriage which divorce brings to an end may have been more so," Dr. Despert writes.

Dr. Richard Gardner, in *Boys and Girls Book About Divorce*, writes: "The child living with unhappily married parents more often gets into psychological difficulties than one whose mismatched parents have been healthy and strong enough to sever their troubled relationship."

We also know that children are less fragile than we think.

Given a foundation of natural endowment and loving care in their earliest years, most children can come through hardships, disappointments, even tragedy, relatively unscarred. There is an inner push in children toward healthy growth that, despite traumatic events, can carry them into adulthood without permanent damage.

In the long run the severance of a life-destroying marriage can be the beginning of a healing and strengthening process not only for the parents but for the children as well. But until the pain and bleeding stop and the shock wears off, everyone is bound to suffer.

2
FATHERING

What does it mean to be a father in today's world? The authoritarian, patriarchal father is a remnant of a bygone era, as outmoded as the buggy whip. With the passing of this concept of fatherhood, many contemporary fathers have been left unsure of their role and uncertain of their place in their children's development.

In our contacts with fathers, we encountered a wide variety of opinions as to what being a father meant. Here are some of the things fathers told us:

> "The mother is the most important person in a child's life."
>
> "My role is to see that my kids have some of the opportunities I didn't have."
>
> "I want to be the kind of father my son can come to when he has a problem, not like my father."
>
> "I began to feel like a father when my kids were old enough to do things with. Holding a baby in my arms didn't make me feel like a father."
>
> "The father's role—he's got one job—is to work and bring home the money to take care of his family."
>
> "It's up to the father to see that the kids toe the mark, that they behave."

All these fathers, telling it as they see it, are giving bits and pieces of fatherhood. Fatherhood is an insufficiently understood and undervalued role. Few fathers realize their significance in the lives of their children or, for that matter, the satisfaction that can be derived from being a father. Until recently, father's nurturing role has been thought of primarily in terms of the economic support he provides for his children. Now more men are beginning to discover the satisfaction that comes from giving comfort and physical care to their offspring.

When Gerald P., our first father, who thought the mother was the all-important figure in a child's life, was challenged to consider what he supplied to his children, he listed first financial support; but as he became more thoughtful, he recalled how his children turned to him with innumerable questions, looking to him for help in understanding the world they lived in. All those whys! Yes, his wife had her share of them all day long, but there were the special ones the children saved for Daddy and the ones they repeated as if they needed confirmation from him. Where does the snow come from? How do airplanes stay in the sky? Why is Mark's skin different from mine? What does God look like? As Gerald reported this, he realized other things he represented for his children. Daddy could be counted on to tell them what was right, what they could do and what they couldn't. Later in the interview he recalled how his three-year-old son had come rushing to his arms in panic when a horse bolted in the park and how he had reassured little Gerald. Describing the scene, he became aware of the child's sense of comfort and protection as he nestled in his father's arms. Surely little Gerald's mother also comforted and protected him. But each parent does it in his own way.

Parenthood is a partnership. In this partnership, Father's unique contribution lies in providing a model of masculine identification for his son. His role in his daughter's development is more subtle. A daughter cannot learn about being feminine from her mother alone—she needs a father, who, by his response to her, confirms her sense of femininity. Father is an integral part of the mother-father constellation that provides the emotional nourishment a child needs to weather the vicissitudes of growing up.

Father and Infant

Much has been written about the vital importance of the mother-child relationship in the first year of life. The foundation of a person's trust and sense of security is laid down then as the mother meets both the physical and emotional needs of the child. These feelings are the basis for the development of self-esteem, an essential element if a child is to mature into an adult able to love, work, and play without too many hang-ups.

It has always been taken for granted that during this period the father contributes indirectly to the child's well-being by giving the mother emotional support—by being loving, patient, comforting—which in turn helps the mother satisfy the infant's needs. (And, of course, there have always been fathers who have participated in the baby's physical care—feeding, giving a bath, changing diapers, and so on.)

But fathers make a more *direct*—and essential—contribution to the child's development. While the helpless infant must be fed, allowed to sleep, and be kept warm and comfortable in order to grow emotionally and intellectually, he also needs the stimulation of close human contact. By their active participation, fathers as well as mothers give the baby that needed stimulation. Fathers enhance the baby's experience with a contact that differs from what the mother provides. When the father holds his infant, it feels different to the child from when the mother holds him. Daddy looks different, sounds different, smells different. He provides the child with variety. A baby needs to hear a deep voice, to sense the way a man handles a child. It's Daddy who swings his child into the air, rides him on his shoulders. See the baby when Daddy walks into the house: the child's face lights up; something new and exciting is being added to his daily routine. Because the infant's experiences with his father and mother differ, he will relate differently to each parent. This early variety enriches the child's capacity for warmth, feeling, and responsiveness to other people.

In the first few months of life, children often show a preference for one parent. When Daddy picks them up, they may whimper; and when they are handed to Mother, they may relax contentedly. If Mother is the preferred parent, many a father interprets this as evidence that he is not important in his child's life at that stage and retreats to fantasies of the time when he will be able to do things with his child—tell him a story, teach him to swim.

Debbie's father found out that he didn't have to postpone his involvement with his daughter. He admitted with some chagrin that when Debbie was three months old she smiled at her mother and was unresponsive to his presence, so that he walked out of the room feeling unnecessary. He felt an intruder. "But I wanted her to know I was there," he reported, "and the next time I was alone with her, even though she didn't smile at me, I started to make babbling sounds, catching her eye, and soon she was smiling at me. Before long she was trying to imitate the sounds I was making. Did I ever get a charge out of that! Now when I come home at night, as soon as she hears my voice, she starts to make these sounds."

The concept of the mother as the primary, all-important figure in the child's early life puts a great burden on women in our society. Even the most maternal woman has periods when she is less able to give of herself than at other times. She may be ill, or tired at the end of the day, or preoccupied with the care of an older child, leaving her little time to attend to the baby. At such times the infant especially needs another parental figure to turn to. Father can help the baby settle down for the night or in other ways give it the comfort and security it might otherwise miss.

The first tooth, the first step, the first word—all the signs of physical and intellectual growth that indicate the child has started on the path of independent functioning—give parents joy. One of the most important steps in a child's development is his increasing awareness that he is a separate individual, apart from his mother. During the second and third years of life, this gradual process erupts into the negativism of the "terrible twos." The *No* so characteristic of the two-year-old is his way of demonstrating that he has a will and a mind separate from his mother's. Often both mother and child have mixed feelings about this independence, each desiring, yet fearing it. Father's presence and his active contact with his child can encourage the child's independence and present a balance, lessening the chances of a child's remaining too tied to his mother.

During the period of "civilizing" the child—of toilet training, of weaning from breast or bottle, of establishing the myriad other restrictions that eventually transform the demanding, self-centered little king of the universe into a social being—Father can participate with Mother, upon whom many of these onerous tasks fall. In so doing he can give his child the opportunity to see that, like Mother, Daddy not only satisfies but also frustrates his needs. Fifteen-month-old Davey enjoys sitting on Daddy's shoulders while he strides around the house. He finds it difficult to accept Daddy's putting an end to the fun, just as he is upset when Mommy says they have to stop their game of "Where's Davey?" because she has other things to do. These experiences help Davey view his parents realistically, ultimately seeing each of them as neither all good nor all bad.

Father and the Preschool Child

As the infant grows into the toddler and nursery-school child, he continues to need the reassurance that he will be taken care of by his parents. Listening to a child's fantasies (which express his wishes), one begins to understand how much the child values his father. In nursery school three-year-old Lisa, whose separated father visits only sporadically, returns from each weekend with reports of how she rode on the back of Daddy's bike or how Daddy took her to his office, when, in fact, Daddy has once again disappointed her and failed to visit at all. Lisa is indicating how much she wants her father's interest and attention and needs it to feel good about herself, as her friend Dickie indicates when he says, "My Daddy is the bestest—he can fix everything." These children are telling us how much they crave paternal care and protection.

At about age three or four, boys and girls develop strong possessive feelings for the parent of the opposite sex. Long before Sigmund Freud formulated his concept of the Oedipus complex, little girls were saying, "When I grow up I'm going to marry my Daddy." This desire for Daddy's all-encompassing love plays an important part in a child's development. A father's attitude and response to his daughter's possessiveness can profoundly affect her feelings about herself as a female and influence her later relationships with the opposite sex. Four-year-old Martha was quite outspoken in her plans for eliminating her mother so that she could be Daddy's wife. Ultimately, of course, she resigned herself to the impossibility of this age-old daydream. Daddy was able to convey to her that while he loved her dearly and could understand how angry she felt toward her rival, she had another equally valued role—she was his daughter whom he loved for herself. From her father's attitude a little girl develops feelings of worth and acceptance of herself as a female. If Daddy is loving to his daughter, she will feel pride in her femininity and in her value as a person.

In turn, little boys of this age become resentful of their father's closeness with Mother. They regard him as a rival for Mother's affection and often become openly antagonistic toward him. The little boy has to learn how to handle his wish to have Mother for himself, his desire to eliminate his competitor, and his fear of both his own and his father's anger. Father's involvement with his son, his acceptance of him with all his rivalrous and angry feelings, will assist him through this phase. The little boy can be helped to reconcile himself to the fact that, though he cannot be Daddy, he can be like Daddy. Having Daddy as a model strengthens the child's pride in himself as a man and helps him handle his loving and competitive feelings, giving him a sound preparation for adult relationships and family life. A tender, loving father helps his son accept his own tender feelings, enabling him to become a richer, more fulfilled person.

Father and the School-Age Child

Just as childhood is a period of development and maturation, so fatherhood is an evolving role. As changes occur in the child, there are accompanying shifts in the father's functioning in order to meet the child's different needs. The strong emotions of the earlier Oedipal period quiet down by the time a child is six or seven. The child is now ready to involve himself with the business of learning about the world, both in and out of school. His horizons are expanding. He is involved in acquiring new friends, new skills. The world is opening wide for him as he learns to read and write, and with these developments come absorbing interests and enthusiasms, from baseball to ancient history. While the child is discovering life outside his home, his father's role takes on another dimension. In addition to being a protector and a model of manliness for both boys and girls, the father becomes the transmitter of social, cultural, and ethical values; he helps the child learn what the world is about. By his actions a father shows his child how to deal with the world and passes on to him, deliberately or unconsciously, his concept of what he considers of first importance.

Father and the Adolescent

In the continuum from infancy to adulthood, the adolescent phase stands out as the bête noire. This erratic, explosive, volatile stage, with its rebelliousness, disparagement of parents, mood swings, and self-centeredness, bewilders and frightens parents. Many a father, finding himself with a child who is an embodiment of incomprehensible contradictions, tries to resolve the dilemma by becoming a pal to his teenager. Or he withdraws with the attitude that "when he rejoins the human race, I'll be able to talk to him; until then he'll just have to work things out on his own."

A father can make a very definite contribution at this stage in his child's development. Perhaps the most striking feature of adolescence is the young person's intense need to be freed from dependency on the parents—to find an identity and eventually establish herself or himself as an adult. In the march toward independence, adolescents desperately need a father with whom they can disagree, yet upon whom they can rely for firmness and limits. As an adolescent seesaws from one mood to another, careening off into fantasies of unfettered independence, then retreating into childish dependency, his anxiety and fears can be mastered if he feels reassured that in asserting himself he will neither destroy nor be destroyed.

Boys at this stage often become very hostile to their fathers. They become particularly adept at spotting a father's weaknesses and shortcomings. When faced with a barrage of crisicism, a father needs a great deal of tolerance, forbearance, and humor to accept the onslaught and to recognize his importance in his son's life. Glenn W. felt battered by his son Donald's constant criticisms and unerring ability to point up inconsistencies in his behavior. One day Donald let Glenn read one of his English assignments—an autobiography. Glenn was amazed to find that Donald had devoted four pages to describing his father's childhood and extolling him for the obstacles he had overcome. (Donald mentioned his mother in two lines.) This glimpse of the other side of the coin revealed to Glenn his importance to Donald as a model. For the first time he understood Donald's rebelliousness against him as the boy's way of trying to fashion his own identity, which in the long run would most likely include those aspects of his father's personality he most admired and treasured.

From infancy through adolescence the father functions as a provider, a protector, and a model both for a son and a daughter of how a man acts and feels. He gives emotional support to the helpless infant and the struggling adolescent. He transmits his ideas and values to his children. Through his love and acceptance a father bolsters his child's self-esteem and concept of himself. But fatherhood is not a one-way street. Nurturing children, watching them grow, seeing their personalities unfold, participating in the development of their characters, encouraging their abilities, sharing their triumphs and disappointments—all this enriches a father's being, enhances his own development, and gives added meaning to his life.

3

PART-TIME FATHERING

When a man is divorced from the mother of his children and leaves home, he assumes a new role with a new title—part-time father. How can a part-time father function as a father when he is no longer in the home? How can he supply the security, the protection, the emotional support, the discipline, that are such important dimensions of fathering? What happens to the father-child relationship? How can he enjoy the pleasures of fathering when he sees his children only once or twice a week? Or less.

Once a Father Always a Father

Actually, the term "part-time father" is a misnomer. Once you are a father, you are always a father. As a result of the divorce, you are in a different position than if you were living with your children, but your departure from the home never abrogates your parenthood. This is a relationship that goes on as long as you live. No one can take fatherhood away from you. You can lose it only by default.

Every part-time father must make his peace with the painful fact that he is no longer a full-time father. This condition is especially hard on the father who had been actively involved in the care and upbringing of his children, who found deep satisfaction in watching them grow and develop. Such a man feels terribly deprived by his circumscribed contact with the children. As one father put it, "What I find hardest to take is seeing my boys only once a week. I miss all sorts of things—being there to help them with their homework or with their practicing, even nagging them to take the dog for a walk. I wouldn't have believed it, but I find that I miss being interrupted in the middle of reading a book to settle a quarrel between the two of them. There's no question about it, you don't get it all, not the good or the bad."

As a part-time father you have to get used to a new pattern of family life. Your basic responsibilities haven't changed, but you have to meet them within a different framework. The transition to this new pattern can be very hard on both father and child (and mother, too, of course). Some men are so overwhelmed by the difficulties that sooner or later they give up. Most men, however, try to make it work, and most of them manage to keep the relationship with their children going in this new setting. It takes a strong desire to remain a father, coupled with a heroic commitment of time and effort—heroic because of the obstacles sometimes set up not only by the mother but also by the children themselves. A father who has left the home should anticipate some trouble with the children, no matter how good and loving the relationship had been before.

The Absent Father and the Young Child

The absence of the father has a different meaning to a child at each stage of his development. The infant may be adversely affected because the mother, preoccupied with her own unhappiness, may be unable to give the baby more than minimal care. The child may become whiny, crying for attention; the pace of his development may be slowed. A young father, recovering from the emotional battering of divorce, often makes the mistake of assuming that his absence at this period of his child's life can have little effect on the baby. When the child is older, he consoles himself, he will participate in his life. He doesn't realize that in turning away from his child he is adding to the infant's deprivation. By continuing to see his child, difficult though this may be, he can provide some of the care and stimulation the baby may be lacking.

The three-year-old may experience Father's absence as an acute loss and may react to it by regressive behavior. He may start soiling himself, develop eating or sleep disturbances, or have temper tantrums. It is important that the father as well as the mother understand that this is the child's way of expressing his anxiety and grief. To punish him for this babyish behavior can only add to his disturbance. A child who feels abandoned by one parent may cling to the other parent all the more. A mother, struggling with her own sense of loss, may turn to the child for her own gratification and may unconsciously encourage the child's dependency to gratify her own unmet needs. By continuing to see his young child as often as possible, the father can serve as a buffer against the child's becoming irrevocably locked into a mutually dependent relationship with his mother.

If the separation occurs during the Oedipal period (which generally starts during the third or fourth year of life), a little boy may experience his father's leaving as a fulfillment of his dream that he has finally gotten rid of his rival for Mommy's love. But this is not sheer bliss for the young suitor. He may interpret Daddy's absence as punishment for his wishes and be beset by guilt and anxiety. The father can help his young son by seeing him regularly during this period, thus allaying his anxiety that Father is dead or has abandoned him in retaliation for his victory.

The little girl whose father leaves home at this stage may also feel that she is being punished for her wishes. She may experience Father's leaving as his rejection of her and as proof that she is unlovable. Or she may prefer to think of her mother as the bad one who drove her beloved father away. The continuing presence of the separated or divorced father in his daughter's life will help her handle these irrational feelings.

The father who continues to be involved with his children after he has left home may find it rough going. He has to be prepared to receive his children's angry as well as loving feelings. His consolation during this trying period comes from knowing that by his acceptance of their anger as well as their love he is helping his children come to terms with their ambivalent feelings. This is a necessary and crucial step in every child's development. It is a particularly difficult one for many children of divorce. In an intact family situation, there is a tomorrow in which to reconcile parent-child blow-ups. The child's love for the parent, momentarily swept away in the storm of anger, surges up again in a loving embrace. He learns in the course of time that he can love and hate the same person, and that hating the loved one does not bring down God's wrath upon his head. Not so for the child of divorce. He does not always have the opportunity to "kiss and make up" after a fracas with the visiting father. Father may himself have to be on his way, or, angry, stalk out of the house, not to return until the next visitation, leaving the child to cope with his angry feelings alone.

How can a part-time father help his child deal with his hostility? The answers are not easy, but being aware of the problem may alert him to situations in which both father and child can get angry with each other without injuring their relationship. If Father must leave before they have patched up their differences, and the visit ends on a sour note, Father will want to call the child as soon as possible to relieve him of his bad feelings and to help him feel loved and loving again.

The Absent Father and the School-Age Child

The grade-school child no longer needs his father with the same intensity as the younger child. Busy learning new skills, making friends, trying himself out in the world outside his immediate family, he becomes less dependent on parents and home. Nonetheless, he experiences a painful loss at his father's absence. Not infrequently, his school work is impaired and he becomes depressed and withdraws from his playmates. Children at this stage are acutely sensitive to the opinions of their peers, especially in regard to their families, and may feel stigmatized by the divorce.

Consistent contact with Father will reassure the child that he has not been deserted and that he can fall back on paternal support, should he need it. Reassured, he can march ahead toward mastering the tasks of middle childhood.

The Absent Father and the Adolescent

Teen-agers caught in the vortex of their struggle with emerging sexual drives and the search for identity and independence need the refuge of home and family. It may be a refuge they rebel against, but its existence gives them a strengthening security to hang onto in their floundering.

Intellectually, adolescents can accept the need for divorce and may even express surprise that it didn't happen sooner. But when Father leaves the family, their concept of home is rudely shaken. The adolescent boy may find himself the man of the house, an ill-fitting role that threatens to revive his earlier longing for Mother, while the adolescent girl may feel abandoned by the father who acted as a cushion in her competitive struggle with her mother. It is unsettling, to say the least, for an adolescent to cope with his own turmoil against the background of a father's departure. A father's continuing involvement with his teen-age children can provide them with some of the guidelines and supports they need during this difficult stage of development.

When to Seek Expert Help

Most children, given time, will adjust to the new family situation. But there are some children who will indicate to you, by the persistence of their symptoms, by their continuing anger or depression, that they need professional help in coming to terms with this alteration in their lives. This does not mean that you or your ex-wife has failed as a parent. Children of all ages often find it easier to talk over their troubles and face their problems with someone who is not a part of the overall picture. Arranging for professional help may be the best thing you can do for them at this critical period.

Divorced Fathers Are Different

Just as there are many kinds of divorces, there are different kinds of divorced fathers. There are divorced men who, freed from the unbearable strain of an unhappy marriage, find their relationship with their children improved. Unshackled from the ties of an unhappy marriage and no longer seeking escape from their emotional dissatisfactions, they are able to give of themselves more freely to their children and to enjoy them at last.

Some men, on the other hand, find the change very hard to take. They do not slip comfortably into this new role. They feel strained and uneasy with the children, and the desire to be a part of their lives gradually gets whittled away. They begin to question their importance to their children. Tom G. was such a father. He and his wife had been separated for six months. In the beginning he had felt very strongly that even though his relationship with his wife hadn't worked, it didn't mean that he couldn't continue to be a father to his eight- and ten-year-old children. Then he began to question this, to wonder if he could really be a father without daily contact with them. Troubled and bewildered, wondering why he felt so uncomfortable when he was with Hilary and Tony, he counted up the hours he spent with them and to his surprise discovered that he spent more time each week with his children than he had spent before he left home. He began to realize that it wasn't the amount of time they spent together but how he and Hilary and Tony felt that was altering their relationship. In trying to understand what was happening, Tom recalled that when he and Lucy told Tony they were going to get a divorce (they had decided to tell each child separately), Tony had been extremely matter of fact. He had asked no questions but seemed eager to get out of the room. Then they heard him rush to his sister's room calling out, "The most terrible thing has happened. Mommy and Daddy are getting a divorce. Who will take care of us?"

"Who will take care of us?"—this cry of anguish had haunted Tom G. during all the months of the separation. Try as he might to reassure the children of his continuing love and interest in them, he felt that he was constantly being challenged by an unspoken, skeptical "Prove it." This, he realized, was creating the chief barrier to the three of them feeling comfortable with one another.

This attitude of skepticism is one many fathers come up against in varied forms. If you love me, why are you leaving me? How can I believe that you will continue to care for me? If you stopped loving Mommy, how do I know you won't stop loving me? the child asks reproachfully, either out loud or inside himself. If a child can express these feelings, the father is fortunate, because then he can deal with them directly. The father who is able to reassure his child of his abiding love has made a step toward reinforcing a faltering relationship. Words, however, are seldom enough. Only as the child experiences again and again the consistency and reliability of his father's concern will he finally be reassured.

Even though children may verbalize their anxieties, they may continue to test their fathers. Many fathers find themselves in a state of confusion as they receive conflicting messages from a child. Molly is bubbling with enthusiasm as she discusses plans for the weekend with Daddy on the phone; but when they get together, to his surprise and disappointment Daddy finds himself with a distant, demanding ten-year-old. Children who are excessively testing and seeking constant proof of Father's love and interest, can never really be satisfied, for they are expressing an unrealistic need to have their father with them always. If the father understands the meaning of such behavior, he will be able to avoid the pitfall of trying to satisfy an insatiable demand. Instead, he will try to respond to the unexpressed and inexpressible anxiety that prompts this behavior—to the children's pain at his absence that is making them distrustful and demanding of constant proof of their father's love. It is to be hoped that the affection and closeness a father enjoyed with his children before he left home will eventually re-emerge as the children become convinced of the dependability of their father's interest.

Many a father, faced with a child who rejects his interest or denies any feeling for him, is tempted to withdraw, rationalizing that the child will be happier without him. Such a father fails to recognize that the divorce has not altered the child's need for him, but that the anger at what he experiences as his father's desertion has sharpened his need for evidence of his father's love and concern. You can meet this need not by words or heroic deeds, but by making yourself available to your child so that he knows he can reach you if he wants to share a success or a disappointment or just craves the reassurance of your hello. The father who drops out of his children's lives may be unaware of the effect of his disappearance on them. The fantasies they weave of the absent father may make him into a superman with a halo or into a devil. If the myth cannot be measured against the reality, the child's now unrealistic image of the father may be lifelong and even color the relationship with other men.

Father's Reactions

The separated or divorced father has to contend not only with the fears and anxieties of his children, but with his own mixed feelings as well. The disruption by divorce of an established pattern of life threatens father as well as child. Facing a new life, looking back upon a marriage that has failed, many a man finds his feelings of relief and release tempered by anxiety at what the future may hold.

For many fathers the greatest fear is that their children may abandon *them*. Feeling insecure, troubled by a sense of loss and emotional emptiness, and driven by his own need for love and reassurance, the father may make inappropriate emotional demands on his children, seeking assurance from them, rather than giving it. In his loneliness, feeling deprived by his loss of daily contact with his children, many a father presses too hard. He may insist on nightly calls, anticipating a long, chatty visit with his children over the phone. Instead he may be met by monosyllabic reticence, ending in a rushed "Gee, Pop, I've got to go." Pop gets off the phone feeling rejected and dejected. "He's on the phone with his friends for hours, how come he can't talk to me?" Perhaps Pop ought to give some thought to his son's situation. He may have forgotten his own youth and how normal it is for children to turn away from their parents and toward their contemporaries. Moreover, a child may feel he is being disloyal to Mother if in her presence he indicates through his manner and tone a closeness to his father. If, as an absent father, you don't approach such calls with your own need to be reassured by your children of their interest in *you*, you will be better able to handle a transitory or seeming rejection. No matter how brief or matter-of-fact the call, you know that you have made contact with them and let them know of your interest. This should be reassuring to all of you.

Father's Guilt

There is scarcely a divorced father who does not feel guilty for inflicting on his children the trauma of a broken home. Guilt is an octopus. In an attempt to avoid its widespread tentacles, fathers often resort to behavior that is counterproductive to their basic aim of maintaining a warm relationship with their children. All too familiar is the father who feels he must make it up to his children by giving them "things" or by countenancing behavior of which he silently disapproves. If he is overpermissive or if his only contacts with his children are fun-filled sprees, they may get a skewed picture of fatherhood, associating it with a life free of frustration. Such an image can foster an unrealistic sense of masculine omnipotence in the young child, poor preparation for later relationships with the opposite sex.

Some separated or divorced fathers are afraid that if they show any displeasure at their child's behavior or discipline him, the child will be angry with them. Ed F. felt as if he were walking on eggs with Randy, who was sullen and negative when they were together. His patience finally reached the breaking point when Randy's rudeness to a waiter in a restaurant embarrassed Ed. He told Randy how he felt about such bad manners. To his amazement Randy said, "I didn't think you cared how I behaved."

Some separated or divorced fathers have unrealistic expectations of the kind of relationship they ought to have with their children. They expect their children to tell them everything they're thinking and feeling. Fred M., for example, felt that his relationship with twelve-year-old Gordon was a failure because the boy would talk about himself only in the most terse and superficial way. He was much more interested in hearing about his father's childhood experiences or in going to his father's photography studio. Fred not only felt guilty at having left Gordon with his emotionally disturbed mother but was also fearful that his former wife would turn Gordon against him. Hence, he was particularly intent on knowing what the boy was thinking. Fred failed to appreciate the meaning of Gordon's questions about his father's life. In his interest in his father's past and present life, Gordon was attempting to identify with his father. If Fred had been less anxious, he might have remembered that twelve-year-olds look to their fathers as models for identification but that their confidences they share with their peers.

Authority

Some men feel that separation from their children divests them of the right to exercise their authority as a parent. For a father to focus on his loss of authority because he is not in the home is to distort an important element of fatherhood and to take a very narrow view of parental authority. You may not be able to have a voice in your children's day-to-day living or to participate in all of the minutiae that a full-time father is exposed to, but this in no way means that you are deprived of the opportunity to present your children with a strong paternal image. They will absorb this from their contacts with you, from observing the kind of person you are, from your care for and interest in them. If you use your time with them to be a father rather than a social director, so that your children know they have meaning in your life and can confide in you and count on your emotional support and guidance, you will always be a person of authority to them.

We have been talking about the stresses and strains that burden the father-child relationship when father leaves home. The vicissitudes vary with each family situation, depending upon a variety of diverse factors—the age of the child, the relationship between the parents before and after the separation, and the needs of all the individuals involved, not least of whom is the ex-wife, who, whether you like it or not, as the children's mother is always somewhere in the picture.

Ex-Wife as Kin

One problem the part-time father has to cope with is how to make the most of what he "gets" with his children. For this he needs the cooperation of his kin by marriage: his children's mother. The concept of kinship has been neglected in the relationship of divorced parents. Through the mixture of their genes in their children, a man and woman become kinsmen. They may be warring kin, but they share a common purpose—their interest in the development and education of their children. Divorce does not cancel that common goal. If both parents recognize the children's need for a father, the two should be able to work out some way for the father to have a good relationship with the children despite the parents' hostile feelings. In a group of divorced mothers discussing their problems, one said, "Ben was a louse to me. But he was a good father, I'll have to admit that. He loves the kids and they love him. Even though he doesn't always come across with the support money, I don't think that's a reason he shouldn't see them when he wants to." Whether cooperation from the custodial parent is forthcoming or not, every divorced father has to solve the problem of arranging matters in a way that permits him to share in his children's growth at the same time he is making a new life for himself.

When to Give Up

There are rare unhappy situations in which the mother, driven by her own needs, will deny the separation agreement and fight court orders in her frantic attempt to literally lock the father out, to eradicate him from the children's lives. This inevitably involves the children in highly charged emotional scenes. The father feels sure their mother is brainwashing them. He may feel, and rightly, that their mother may intercept his letters and gifts or thwart any attempt on his part to continue his link with his children. He wants desperately to remain a part of their lives: he knows that after a brief period they can be happy with him. Yet when he sees his children tense and trembling, torn by the pull to each parent, he is in a quandary. Is the situation so intense, so resistant to conciliation, that he should consider temporarily withdrawing from their lives in order to reduce the pressure on them? This is a painful question; the solution may be painful too. But perhaps, in the best interests of the child, such withdrawal is the only viable choice. And perhaps, at a later period, when the children are older, he may be able to explain his decision and resume the contact he has relinquished with such anguish.

4
HARRY—ONE DIVORCED FATHER

Before going on to the grueling day-to-day aspects of divorce and children—breaking the news to them, custody, visiting, support, remarriage, new families—let us look in on Harry Smith, a fictional composite of many part-time fathers. His experience gives us an insight into the lives of divorced fathers.

Harry Smith braced himself against the blustery March wind as he hurried along the park, hunching his head between his shoulders and pulling up his coat collar. Harry was on his way to visit his children, Bobby, eight, and Barbra, six. It was his Saturday-morning ritual for the past year and a half.

As he neared the street where they lived, his pace slowed. He was eager to see his kids, but he found himself, as he did before every visit, reluctant to enter his former home. Six months had passed since he and Ann had been divorced, but the same nagging thoughts that had hounded him from the moment of separation—it seemed a lifetime ago—still continued to plague him. Had he done right to agree to the divorce? Could he have tried harder to patch things up? Should he have given in and gone to a marriage counselor, as Ann had begged him to do? Had he harmed the children by leaving? Would they hold it against him when they grew up? He would never know.

He consoled himself, as he did whenever his worry about the children made him anxious and filled with guilt, with the clichés his friends sympathetically canted. Children are better off with divorced parents than with life in an atmosphere of discord and marital unhappiness. Actually, Harry, they would remind him, you can be a better father, see more of them than when you were living at home but staying away nights working late or drinking with the boys. He recalled weekends nursing hangovers, being irritable and cranky, yelling at the children if they made so much as a peep. He whipped himself with the recollection of hitting Bobby brutally once when the child's ball inadvertently struck him while he was trying to take a snooze on the terrace. Yeah, the kids are better off—

But these arguments never convinced him. Don't kid yourself, Harry, he confronted himself. The truth is you were so damn crazy about that two-timing bitch Marilyn, you couldn't think or care about anyone else, not even your kids. You thought you could get away with it, have your cake and eat it too. Well, now you know. After Ann found out (How the hell did she find out? Some treacherous friend?), you did try for a while. You really tried. There was the reconciliation, the vows, the promises (unkept—you couldn't get that bitch out of your mind), the lies, the recriminations, and—finally—the ultimatum. Some women close their eyes to these things, look the other way. But not Ann; prim, puritanical Ann. Give her up or get out, she demanded. So you got out. You really didn't expect Ann to go through with the divorce. You were sure she'd take you back. But she didn't. Let's face it, Harry. You traded in two innocent children and a faithful wife of ten years for a piece of ass, a piece you were sure you couldn't live without, who left you two weeks later.

As always in his ruminations, self-justification followed self-flagellation. The marriage had turned sour long before Marilyn came along, he assured himself. Ann had turned into one awful nag. If he poured himself so much as an extra Scotch after dinner, like a broken record it was always, "Harry, don't you think you're drinking too much?" And God help him if he really had a good time at a party. Stony silence on the ride home. Long, accusing face when they got to the house. Then, getting ready for bed, the outburst. "You sure made a fool of yourself with that floozy Lorraine. Why do you have to humiliate me in public?" Accusations, tears, reminders of "sins" committed years past—ending up with his taking a blanket and sleeping on the couch.

And the constant arguments about money. He was really quite a generous man, he told himself, never questioned her about where the money went. But there never seemed to be enough for her, even though for a man of his age he was making a darned good salary. Not that Ann was extravagant exactly, he admitted to himself, except maybe when it came to her clothes. But why was it that friends who earned no more than he seemed to manage so much better?

And then there was Bertha, her mother, her bossy, loud-mouthed, interfering mother. Oh, come off it, Harry, he chided himself. Everybody's got mother-in-law troubles. You know it wasn't Bertha or the money or the nagging that finally did the marriage in. It wasn't even Marilyn. Why don't you admit it? It was—well, there just wasn't anything between you any-more, not even in bed. You couldn't understand what happened. You still can't. She had been so loving, so responsive, so eager before you were married. And for the first year or two after.

It started going bad after Bobby came. It was okay when the doctor said no sex for a month—something about complications after the Caesarean. In fact, he had felt more tender, more protective—like a good father to her. Then, afterward, she was tired all the time. Taking care of the baby, the house, the meals, the laundry—too tired, she claimed, when he tried to make love. When she did give in, hell, she made him feel like a rapist or some kind of brute.

After Barbra came, they made love less and less often. On several occasions, when she did finally turn to him and make advances, he found he couldn't respond. He assumed it was his fault—maybe his glands were drying up—he had read about that in a magazine when he was a boy. The thought of being through at thirty-five worried and depressed him. Without Ann's knowledge he consulted a doctor. The doctor found nothing physically wrong—he suggested a psychiatrist. (A shrink! Did Doc think he was nuts?) Then along came Marilyn—lusty, fun-loving Marilyn. You bet there was nothing wrong with him! Marilyn restored his confidence in his virility, and a rash of brief affairs following their breakup confirmed it. It was only with Ann that he had flopped as a man, so it must have been her fault all along, he reassured himself. But all his rationalizations about the breakup never stilled for long his heartache over leaving the children.

The building where Bobby and Barbra were waiting for him loomed in the near distance, shaking him from his ruminations. What would he do with the kids today? Ann called yesterday to say Bobby had a cold, and if his temperature wasn't down this morning, he couldn't go out. In a way Harry would be relieved. It would be nice to lounge around the house with the kids on such a miserable day, like old times, playing chess with Bobby or maybe just watching television. If only Ann would leave him alone with the children—go shopping, or visit her mother. The few times he had stayed in with them, she had hovered in the background, her flitting presence an unspoken reproach. Still, it would be better than dragging them to a museum again and eating at Howard Johnson's.

It was always a problem knowing what to do with the children. At first it was fun going to museums, showing off his knowledge of fossils and prehistoric beasts, telling them about the Indians and pointing out their crafts. Or visiting the zoo and buying peanuts for the kids to feed the elephant; or wandering through department stores and loading them with gifts. Or taking them to a movie (it was getting harder and harder to find one fit for kids) and afterward eating hot dogs or pizza and treating them to a double hot-fudge sundae just before they went home. Sometimes he would take the children to visit his widowed mother. It was always a treat for her to see them. But after the affectionate greetings and the mutual pleasure of stuffing and being stuffed with goodies, there was nothing for the kids to do, and in a while they would get restless and bored and nudge him to leave.

He was running out of ideas. The first six months or so after he left home he scarcely saw the children—only once in a while and then just for an hour or two in the house. Ann discouraged his visits at that time; said it upset them for days afterward. He himself thought it didn't matter much to them, they were so young and so attached to their mother. It wasn't really until after the divorce—he shuddered at the memory of all the fighting and haggling and squabbling about alimony and child support and visitation rights written out in the contract—that he began to see the children regularly, partly out of duty but partly, he had to admit, because he missed them.

Of course, when there was something special in town, like the circus or a ball game or a puppet show, it was easy. But those were bonanzas that happened only once in a while. It would be nice just to take them to his place, sit around like old times when he was in a relaxed mood, ask them about their school and friends and what they'd been doing. Maybe send out to Jolly Chan's for some chow mein and fried shrimp—the kids loved that—and have a feast. He had tried bringing them to his apartment once or twice during the legal separation, but it hadn't worked out very well. They wandered around the little flat timidly, a little suspiciously, their eyes lighting up only when they chanced upon some old recognized possession—their picture on his dresser or the silver cup he won at college for the broad-jump record. And they spoiled it all by their questions, their childish, irritating questions: How long are you going to stay here, Daddy? When are you coming home? Why don't you love Mommy anymore? Do you love us, Daddy? He would try to explain, patiently, lovingly, to reassure them—Daddy will always love you—but his answers never seemed to satisfy them. In a little while they would begin again with their stupid questions, and he would become annoyed and unable to hide his irritation.

Now, since Elaine had moved in with him, he couldn't take

them home anyway. Her presence would be too difficult to explain. Remembering Elaine, his thoughts jumped to the summer. When the court granted him the right to have the children for a month during the summer, he had been pleased. He imagined how enjoyable it would be—he and the children in a cottage by the sea. Or perhaps it would be nicer in the mountains; take them trout fishing in a stream. Now he wasn't so sure. Elaine expected him to spend his vacation with her. How would it work out if he took the children along? Would she mind? Would they like her? What would Ann say? His thoughts about summer plans were in a jumble. Well, he'd have to cross that bridge when he came to it.

Speaking of girl friends, he wondered who the Uncle Charlie was that the kids mentioned last week had come to the house for dinner. Some guy taking Ann out, he figured. Man, wouldn't it be great if she got married again? No more alimony, only child support. Maybe he could move into a bigger apartment. Or get himself a Volkswagen so he could take the kids out to the country on Saturdays now that spring was coming.

If Ann married again—that meant the kids would have a stepfather. A stepfather! Supposing he was some mean son-of-a-bitch who would push Bobby around. Or be harsh to Barbra. If he touches so much as a hair on my kids' heads, I'll break every bone in that bastard's body. Charlie. Who did he know named Charlie? There was Charlie Gallagher, big, handsome Chuck, all-star track man at college. The girls used to go gaga over him. Even Ann, when she met Chuck once at Harry's class reunion, joked about how Chuck could put his shoes under her bed any day. No, couldn't be Charlie Gallagher. Harry recalled that Charlie was married about the same time he was. Still, Chuck could have gotten a divorce too. Plenty of men his age do. He imagined Chuck playing ball with Bobby, holding Barbra on his lap and stroking her hair, bringing presents home to both of them. Maybe they would like Chuck better than him, their own father. That's what kids are like these days. Ungrateful. Out for what they can get.

Harry caught himself. Harry, you off your rocker? Here you've got Ann married and the kids with a stepfather and you out in the cold, just because you hear about a guy named Charlie. Watch yourself, man—

Harry arrived at his former home, entered the foyer, and rang the bell. . . .

Part II

NITTY-GRITTY OF DIVORCE

5
BREAKING UP

The worst time in the whole painful business of divorce, many men tell us, is the weeks and months before the actual breakup of the family. There will be other miserable periods after you've taken that final step out the door: the meetings in lawyers' offices while legal arrangements are contrived (and often connived); the charges and countercharges; the haggling over money and who gets what; the quibbling over custody and visiting rights. But neither the physical nor the financial hardships, nor even the loneliness and guilt and uncertainties that follow the breakup of the marriage, can compare in misery to the ceaseless gnawing at your innards while gathering the strength to leave home—and the children—for good.

"Looking back," recalls Bruce T., now happily remarried, "the worst time for me in that whole miserable business of getting divorced was that period after Pam and I decided we just couldn't make it together anymore but before I actually packed my bags and left. Funny, at the time I worried more about telling the kids that Pam and I were splitting up—though I'm sure now they knew something was wrong, since I was sleeping on the living-room couch—than I did about leaving them. Of course, I didn't realize then how much they meant to me or how much I'd miss them. All I could think of was my own unhappiness. I felt my life was going down the drain. I couldn't stand the constant wrangling with Pam over every little thing or seeing that martyred, reproachful look on her face when we weren't fighting. Or endure my own guilt at somehow, without knowing how or why, having turned that girl, whom I thought so sweet and lovable when I married her eight years ago, into this hateful, shrieking harridan. Or myself into a yelling, irritable grouch. There wasn't 'another woman' in the picture, or, as far as I know, 'another man.' It was just that our marriage had sickened and died. If I was not to be buried with it, if I was to save myself, and Pam and the kids too, I had to go. Not that I expected strawberries and cream out there. But anything seemed better than the hell I was going through.

"It was easier said than done. When I thought of actually leaving, I found myself filled with unendurable anxiety. Doubts and uncertainties. . . . Terrible feelings of guilt. . . . I lost my appetite. I developed headaches and couldn't sleep without pills. My work fell down, though I stayed at the office longer than ever. My colleagues began to notice and inquire after my health. Even my boss suggested I take a vacation.

"By then, of course, Pam and I were scarcely talking to each other. And I hardly ever saw the kids, since I'd have my dinner out and come home after they were in bed. But every time I promised myself that tomorrow I'd rent a room in a residential hotel near the office—eventually I did and stayed for a couple of months until I found an apartment—I'd find some excuse for putting it off. It was Pam who finally ended my shilly-shallying. If I didn't leave the house by next week, she warned, she would. I could hear from the steel in her voice that it was an ultimatum. It was the best thing she could have done for me, for all of us. I left the next day."

Breaking Up and the Children

The breaking-up period is one of the worst for the children, too. To hear parents scream at each other, to see their faces distorted in rage and hatred—this is a grueling experience for children of all ages. For young children it is particularly terrifying. Little children are self-centered. They see and interpret what goes on in the household, especially where parents are concerned, in terms of themselves. They think it is their fault when parents fight, that it's because they were "bad." In the dark recesses of their imaginations they conjure up far more terrible consequences than the most dire reality. Many symptoms of early childhood—like night terrors or fear of the dark or of animals, even temper tantrums—often stem from a child's fantasies of horrors that await him for being bad. Little children believe that "bad" thoughts—like wishing a brother or sister would die or disappear—as well as being naughty, can make parents no longer love or protect them. Observe a three-year-old playing with her doll. "Be a good girl," she warns dolly, "or Daddy will go away." Or, "Bad dolly. I'm going to spank you. Now Daddy won't love you. He is going to leave you all alone."

Even when parents make a conscious effort to hide their discord—"Let's behave like civilized human beings in front of the children"—children are not fooled. They see the reddened eye, the bitten lip, the glowering look. They hear the tight voice, the overpolite manner. Like some small, wary creature sensing danger, they feel tense and frightened. They misread in their parents' preoccupation with their own troubles signs that they are indeed unloved and unwanted, and they expect some life-threatening disaster to pounce on them or carry them off.

A four-year-old, who used to run happily to fetch his father's briefcase as he left for work each morning and to wave good-by, began to cry and cling to his father, begging him not to go to work that day. The child was presumably ignorant of the parents' decision to separate. But he felt it in his bones.

A ten-year-old girl was referred for treatment because she adamantly refused to leave the house and go to school. In the course of treatment we learned that one night during a "secret" quarrel between her parents, she heard her mother threaten to kill herself. It turned out the child feared that if she left home her mother might carry out the threat, and so she had to stay home to watch over her.

Telling the Children

Children are tougher than we think. They can handle painful realities—after all, that is an essential part of growing up—if they trust the parents, feel they can depend on them, and know exactly where they stand.

Once the decision to separate is final and irrevocable, the children should be told. It is far better for them to know the truth, no matter how painful or upsetting at the time, than to be left to struggle with vague fears and frightening fantasies stirred up by half-truths and evasions.

That's no easy assignment. To witness your child's stricken face or to feel his wrath as you deal him this blow is a terrible thing. No wonder many a departing parent leaves the responsibility to the remaining one—"Tell the children whatever you want"—or postpones the ordeal until the separation is already an accomplished fact. Even after the parent has left, the remaining one may lack the courage to tell the child, especially a very young child, the bald truth. The parent may equivocate, hedge for time with a white lie like "Daddy's gone on a trip" or "Mother went to visit Grandpa." Such tactics usually indicate the parent's own reluctance to accept the separation as final. These evasions only further confuse an already confused child. Double-talk unsettles him even more.

When

How soon should we tell the children? is a question frequently asked. Don't wait until you have one foot out the door. But they needn't be told so far in advance that your continued presence in the home for weeks or months afterward raises in them false hopes that you and your spouse may yet change your minds and you'll stay. Give them enough time, while you are still around, to weather the shock of the breakup of the old Mommy-Daddy combination—and it is always a shock to children when it happens, even when they've been exposed for a long time to fights, threats of leaving, or temporary separations.

Who and What

Ideally, both parents together should tell the children. But perhaps this is expecting more than is humanly possible of two persons whose relationship has eroded to the point of no return. In such situations, each parent has to face this difficult task alone. Try not to "dump" on the other parent. The temptation is almost irresistible, especially with older children, to point out the other parent's defects and to put yourself in a favorable light, particularly if you are the one to be leaving and are afraid of losing the children's love. ("You know yourself what a terrible nag your mother is. Nothing I did was ever right. No matter how much I earned, how hard I worked to give her and you kids everything you wanted, it was never good enough for her. She always tried to make me feel like two cents.") And avoid, if possible, putting them in the untenable position of choosing sides. Children have enough to cope with at this difficult time without having to pass judgment on "who's to blame."

Children are not blind to their parents' faults. They may complain about them, but it does not make them love the parents less—or need them less. It hurts children to hear one parent derogate the other—even when what is said is true. For the sake of the child try to keep untarnished as far as you can the image of the other parent as a good, a decent person, despite his or her faults and despite the fact that the two of you can no longer live together.

What to Tell Them

What you tell the children beyond the stark fact that you and their mother can no longer live together will depend on their age, their emotional maturity, and your particular situation. With divorce so common these days, the chances are that your children have friends or relatives whose parents are divorced. Nonetheless, to each child confronted with divorce in his own life, it is a catastrophic event. Try to be as honest as possible. Without necessarily going into the intimate details of what led to the final breakup of your marriage, let them know—particularly older children—that there are too many things you and their mother disagree over, that the differences between you are too great to be reconciled, that your constant arguing and fighting has made everyone miserable, and therefore you and their mother think it best for all concerned that you and she live apart. Children need something definite to ponder over, to chew on and digest, in order to master and come to terms with this painful "fact of life."

Be prepared for some tough questions, particularly if the child is very young, questions like, "Why don't you love Mommy (or Daddy) anymore?" Behind that question may lurk the more dreaded, though unexpressed one. "Will you stop loving me?" If this comes up, some simple explanation of different kinds of love may be in order. You will want to assure your child that while adults may fall out of love with each other, parents love their children forever. Most important, let them know as precisely as possible what will happen to them now that the family is being disrupted.

First, give them the details about their future everyday existence under the changed circumstances: Be concrete, spell out where they will live, where they will go to school—and for most children this means having the reassurance of remaining in the same house and attending the same school—where you will live, how often you will see them, how they will be provided for, and all the other things they may want to know. One little boy asked if his father's mother would still be his granny.

Be sure to make a definite date for the very next time you will see them or be in touch with them. And give them an address or telephone number at which they may reach you. It is quite understandable that a father, himself in a distraught state at the moment of leaving the children, may not think of the children's need to feel they can reach out to him when they wish to. By giving them something concrete about yourself to hang onto, you give them assurance that you are still an integral part of their lives, even though you will no longer be physically present in the home.

Second, help the children understand that the separation or divorce is from the mother, *not from them.* Although you must leave the house because you and their mother can no longer live together under the same roof, you will always be in touch with them and go on loving them as you always did, no matter where you are.

Third, one cannot stress strongly enough the importance of assuring the children, especially young children, that the decision to separate had nothing to do with them. *It is not their fault.* It is strictly something between Mother and Father.

Along with the fantasy of being responsible for their parents' separation, very young children nourish another common—one might almost say universal—fantasy: by being very, very good or in some other magical way—for example, by depriving themselves of some pleasure—they can keep their parents united. A two-and-a-half-year-old, when told of the impending separation, responded by giving his beloved teddy bear to his hated infant sister. In so threatening a situation as separation from a beloved parent, the belief in the magical power to make good things happen or to undo bad things helps very young children deny their overwhelming feelings of helplessness, of being utterly at the mercy of the adults in charge of them.

Even school-age children may think they are responsible for the separation. They hear their parents fighting about them when trouble arises at school or at home or in the neighborhood. They hear each blame the other for overindulgence or overstrictness or neglect, and it makes them wonder, as does the younger child, if the separation may somehow be their fault.

Fourth, children need the reassurance not only of your continuing love but of your continuing concern for their welfare. Children of divorcing parents worry more than we know about their future. A ten-year-old girl whose parents' battles centered largely—and loudly—on money matters, believed that her father, a well-to-do businessman, would no longer support her and her mother now that he had moved out—they would have to go on welfare. She began hoarding food and stealing coins from her schoolmates' lockers in anticipation of those lean days.

Children's Reactions

Each child reacts to the news of the family breakup in his own way. One child will cry and plead that you remain. "Janet was heartbroken," Walter N. reported, in recounting his experience upon telling his six-year-old daughter of the impending separation. "She kept begging me to stay. 'Don't go, Daddy, don't go,' she kept saying over and over. It tore my heart out." Tears came to his eyes as he recalled the incident, though it had happened the year before. "It broke my heart to see her crying so hard. I felt like I was murdering my own child."

Another (usually a late adolescent) will say, much to the

astonishment of the parent, "It's about time. I don't know how you put up with her for so long." Or try to console you. "When I told Maggie [age eighteen], she said, 'Maybe it's for the best. I know you and Mom never got along. I never understood how two such different kinds of people ever got together in the first place.'"

Another child will hide his grief and remain silent. "I decided to tell Chris [age ten] when I went up to his room to say good night after he was in bed. I told him I had something sad to tell him. His mother and I were separating. He knew we were arguing and fighting all the time and all of us were unhappy, and we thought it was best for everybody if she and I separated since we couldn't seem to live together. Chris didn't say a word. He just turned his back to me and faced the wall. I sat there on his bed for a long time, maybe an hour or more, stroking his hair. He never said anything the whole time, though I tried to get him to talk."

Another will pretend she doesn't care. "When I told Beth, she went on playing with her dolls as though she didn't hear a word I said. Ordinarily she is a regular chatterbox—we call her Miss Chatty—but she didn't say anything except to her dolls. Pretended she didn't care."

No show of feeling—don't be deceived. A child who pretends not to care may be so overwhelmed that he takes flight in silence or denial. However a child reacts—whether with tears, anger, silence, disdain, or pretended unconcern—you may be sure he feels betrayed. The bottom has fallen out of his world. This is particularly true of the young child who is dependent upon his parents for his sustenance, physical and emotional. Even if he says nothing or nods his head sympathetically and says he understands, don't let it go at that. Encourage him to ask questions, give voice to his fears, talk about his concerns, his anger, his accusations. Above all, help him to grieve. The departure of a father and the disruption of the family unit is indeed something to grieve about. This is not an easy thing to do at a time when you yourself feel so abandoned, so full of self-pity or guilt, so vulnerable to attack. It is hard to think of the needs of others when you want and need comfort yourself.

Of course, you will assure the child of your love. But remember: it is hard for him to believe you love him when in actual fact you are leaving him. To the child, your leaving the household—even when it is against your will and the child knows it—means only one thing to him at the time: you are abandoning him. Oddly enough, like the child, most fathers feel the same way: they feel they are being abandoned too.

After Closing the Door

You will want to help your children weather the initial impact of the separation, at least until they have time to absorb the new reality and come to terms with it. Try to remain in close touch with them particularly during the first few weeks—every day, if possible—by telephone, postcard, letter, in person, or in any manner that will convey to them the message they are in your mind. With small children, you may want to give them your picture and show them you carry theirs in your wallet. Make sure they know how to get in touch with you. And always make a date with them for the next time you will be together again.

Some fathers—and some mothers, too—think it is better for the children if father does not see them for a while immediately after the breakup in order to help them accept and adjust to the new family situation. Janet's father (the one who felt like a murderer of his child) wondered whether it wouldn't be a good idea if he didn't see her for a while "so she'll get used to my not being there." One can sympathize with his wish to avoid a repetition of that heartrending experience with his little girl. But his idea seemed more like a rationalization to spare himself, and perhaps Janet, another painful scene.

There are other reasons a father may stay away from the children at the beginning of the separation. This is generally the period when the relationship between the parents is at its nadir—when each is most angry or bitter or vindictive against the other—and contact with the children may mean contact with the embattled or embittered spouse. "Every time I call to speak to Kate," Patrick J. complains, "my wife answers and starts haranguing me again. After one of these calls I feel like I've been hit over the head." No wonder Patrick puts off calling Kate, or forgets to call altogether.

Not infrequently, during this period the mother will forbid the father to see the children either as a weapon of retaliation or out of a genuine belief that it is in the children's interest not to see him, since, as many mothers have told us, the children are upset after a visit with their father. It is quite true that children, particularly young children, after being with Father, often return home in an excited, even feverish state, sometimes unable to eat or sleep. It makes the mother's job of dealing with the children, already disturbed by the upheaval in their lives, all the harder. We believe, however, it is better for the children to see their father as frequently as possible especially during this period of adjustment—even at the cost of their being upset for a while afterward.

Particularly at this crucial time, encourage your children to talk about themselves. Get them to tell you not only what they do but how they feel, even though it may pain you to hear it. And let them know about your life so they won't feel shut out of it. The more you can be in touch with them, in person or by telephone or letter, the more secure and reliable will your relationship become and the sooner will they come to believe that *they* are not being divorced.

6
THE VISITING FATHER

The two thorniest issues in any separation agreement are visitation rights and money. Unfortunately, they are often used interchangeably as bargaining points. As one father said when his ex-wife put further monetary demands on him, "I'm being asked to pay ransom in order to see my children." All too often fathers will fight the settlement, demanding, as if they were negotiating a union contract, longer vacation time, each holiday carefully evaluated, while behind it all runs the leitmotif "I don't want to lose my child."

No matter how desperately a man may want a divorce, one can safely say that almost no father wants to be divorced from his children. No matter how much visiting time the father is allowed by the mother, now officially dubbed "the custodial parent," he invariably feels his parental role is diminished. Before the divorce he may not have seen much of the children. Now he fights for every moment he's legally entitled to.

The separation or divorce agreement gives you the right to see your children. You regard this not only as your right but as your responsibility, and you earnestly want to carry out this responsibility. But you feel as if you're in a straitjacket. The very word "visitation" connotes such rigidity. You can't be spontaneous. Today is a beautiful day, and you'd like to take your boys out and play ball. But it's not your "visitation" day. Last week when it was your day, you had a hangover. You were feeling rotten and grumpy, the kids were irritable, the day was a disaster, and you were miserable all week. How can you pack being a father into such a narrow structure? you wonder. You want to give the children a sense of your belonging together, of still being a part of one another's lives. While your visits with your children give you the chance to do that, there's somehow an air of artificiality hovering over the visits.

Many fathers complain of the difficulties during the first year, when they are trying to adjust to this altered family pattern. Inwardly pressured to make the most of their brief time with the children, they create an aura of tension. They weigh each visit, grade it. If it doesn't come up to expectations—and it seldom does—they are disappointed and depressed; they berate themselves for not having done better. They harbor an unrealistic image of a father who is always with his child. Measured against this ideal, they feel theirs is a hopeless task. So, instead of enjoying the time they do have with their children, they torment themselves that there isn't more of it.

Try to view your time with your child in the context of a long, ongoing relationship that doesn't stand or fall on one visit. As long as you live you will be their father. If you don't approach your visits with the feeling that every moment must count, you will be better able to achieve that warm relationship you had hoped for. Remember that even in the happiest of homes, children and parents have their good times together and their bad times.

Faced with a new situation in which they do not feel comfortable, some people react with excessive activity in an attempt to cope with their anxiety. Thus we find the fathers who turn each visit into a hectic round of movies, shopping sprees, restaurants, and circuses. They wear themselves out in a futile attempt to handle their feelings of strangeness and discomfort.

In the beginning, when you and the children are trying to

find your way in this strange new world (and when you may not yet be settled in a place of your own), public spots and commercial entertainment may be the handiest resources for your getting together. Also, during this period, when you may feel awkward with one another, "going places and doing things" can serve to fend off the very intimacy you will eventually want to re-establish.

In the course of time, as you and your children get accustomed to your altered family pattern, you will want to renew a more relaxed father-child relationship. A routine of movies and dinner in a restaurant is hardly conducive to this. Try doing everyday things with your children that will give them an opportunity to talk, to share their problems. Learn to cook, and let your children help. Play chess, Scrabble, or other games with them, or watch television together.

Don't be surprised if your children, for what seems like no reason at all, become moody or irritable. Perhaps they are recalling the good times you had together as a family—an afternoon of ice skating, a favorite Sunday-night dinner, a vacation at the beach. They have to make their peace with this loss.

Your visits with your children give them an opportunity to see you through their own eyes, not their mother's; to absorb your values; to experience you as a flesh-and-blood father. Give them a chance to find out about the things you are interested in. Share your hobbies with them. If it's possible, take them to your place of work. When your children overcome their anxiety about sharing you, introduce them to your friends and try to meet theirs. At the same time, this will give you the opportunity to learn what stage your children are at, what their current interests and concerns are. You may be expecting a child to write you a note when she is still struggling to write her name. Unwittingly you may make your child feel that she is not living up to your expectations. If you are really clued in, you will know what she is capable of. One of the best ways to find out is by being involved in your children's school—meeting their teachers and going to parents' meetings.

Visits with the Very Young Child

Visits with the children take on different forms not only as time elapses after the divorce but at different stages of each child's development.

For many men, trying to be a father to a baby or toddler when they are no longer living in the home is almost an impossible task. Yet you don't want to lose contact with your child. But how can you become part of a little one's life in a few hours a week or even over a weekend? Moreover, of necessity, visits generally take place in the mother's home. Even without the mother's presence it's a trying, even painful situation for most young fathers.

Taking the child to your place has its problems, too. Adam S., whose daughter Kathy was two when her parents separated, described the ordeal of visiting with her from the vantage point of three years' experience as a divorced father. "She was so little. I hardly knew her. When I was living at home, I was so miserable with Jackie that I jumped on every excuse to be away from the place as much as possible, came home late, the whole bit. But after the divorce, I knew I had to see my child, be with her, even though we were strangers. In fact, once the daily tension of life with Jackie was removed, I began to see myself as more of a father. And even if I had wanted out as a father, I would have had to deal with my parents, who weren't about to give up their first grandchild. I don't know if I could have done it without them, not that there weren't problems there. So there I was, taking Kathy in training pants, clutching her security blanket, to my apartment. It wasn't until much later that I began to understand how much she really needed that blanket. I had pushed the furniture around in my dining alcove, put a crib in the corner, and fitted the room out with all the toys I thought she might like (everything from a Barbie doll to a musical teddy bear)—ready, I thought, for my first sleep-over date with my daughter. It was a miserable visit. There was lots of crying and whining, and some snarling on my part. Only later did I realize that I had been too ambitious, prompted, I'm afraid, by a desire to prove to one and all—Jackie, my parents, and perhaps most of all myself—that I could be a father if not a husband. I never stopped to question whether Kathy was ready for this kind of visit. She scarcely knew me. I had only been a fleeting presence in her life. Besides, she just wasn't ready to be away from her mother for that long a time. It was tough going.

"Looking back, I'd say we both could have been spared a lot of grief had I kept foremost in my mind what was best for her. I should have started out slower, visiting with her for a couple of hours the first few times, not buying out the toy store but just having a couple of duplicates of her favorite toys." As Adam concluded his recital, he summed it up very aptly: "The details wouldn't have mattered if I'd had my eye on the ball—what was best for Kathy. It still holds true, even now, three years later. Problems come up, but I find it easier to face them if I keep what is best for Kathy as my rule of thumb."

Many fathers particularly miss not being able to be with their young child at bedtime. This is the time when a child is generally most open, most receptive to loving; the time when he is ready to share his feelings with Father, the time of special closeness. As Adam learned the hard way, most children under three find overnight separation from the mother frightening, so you'll just have to give up that special pleasure for a while. By the time a child reaches kindergarten age, however, you need no longer be deprived of that experience, unless he is unduly timid or tied to his mother and afraid to be away from her overnight. Then you'll have to wait a little longer.

The Young Child's Sense of Time

To the toddler, separation from Mother for more than the afternoon can be a trying experience. The young child isn't able to anticipate time. Tomorrow, next week, next month, all seem like forever. He needs the father's presence to be reassured that he hasn't disappeared. Frequent visits of short duration may be a happier solution.

If, for instance, his daughter is going to nursery school or a day-care center and if Daddy can manage it, he might pick up his little girl and take her to school or take her home at the end of the day. Having a brief contact like this will help the young child understand that Daddy doesn't disappear or cease to exist from one formal visiting day to another. A useful formula might well be that the younger the child, the more frequent the visits.

With the best will, there are many fathers who can't arrange to follow such a schedule. Much as they would like to reassure their child by their physial presence, they can only be weekend fathers. There are other ways of communicating reassurances and interest. Even the toddler can respond to a few words and the sound of Daddy's voice on the phone, or a brief note saying hello. For the young child, fathers might well take their cue from the style children have responded to over the generations—repetition. Daddy, who can't manage to be with two-year-old Jeb except on a weekly basis, can repeat to him the same way he does his favorite rhymes and stories, "I saw you last week. Today is Sunday. We're together today, and next Sunday we'll take another walk, just as we did today."

In planning for your visits with your children, you will, of course, try to do what they enjoy doing. But only as long as you like it. If your sons like to fish but you find it boring, it's likely that in a little while you'll become impatient and your visit will be a strain. On the other hand, to do only what *you* enjoy doing has its strains too. You can't expect your children to fit into your adult habits. If you like to watch football all Sunday afternoon, don't be surprised if your daughters interrupt your viewing with demands for attention.

Fathers sometimes expect their children to be more mature than is suitable for their age. Following a separation or divorce, a child often falls back on earlier ways of behaving. You may be appalled to find that your eight-year-old is suddenly sucking his thumb again, or that your ten-year-old is back to needing a light when she goes to sleep. Shaming or belittling the child can only worsen things. You'll need understanding and patience until the child feels more secure with you and can give up the crutch.

Changes in Styles of Visits

As your children get older, the visits naturally assume a different character. With your school-age child who has developed a sense of time, you may want to change the style of your visits. Frequent, brief contacts may be unsatisfactory. The older child may need more time to settle in with you, to get over the feeling of strangeness, to make the bridge from his life with Mother to his life with you. A longer weekly visit may be more comfortable. All of this, of course, depends on the quality of your relationship with your children. There are no hard and fast rules; you have to use your common sense. If you and your children feel in touch with one another, you will be able to work out an easy pattern of visiting. As we said earlier, the sleep-over visit that may have been inappropriate for a three-year-old can be managed quite well by the five- or six-year-old. Eight-year-old Larry might enjoy having supper during the week with you; it would give him an opportunity to tell you what happened at school, and then to go home and still have time left for his favorite TV program. Ten-year-old

Sara, who used to resent even a telephone call as an intrusion on her time with you when she was little, is now so at ease with you that she brings her friend to play with her, scarcely paying any attention to you.

At Dad's Place

The tendency of the freshly divorced father is to see his visits with his children as a special event. Lacking the ease that daily contact with children brings, he may tend to treat them as if indeed they were guests in his home. Whether the time spent together is a few hours or a month during vacation, both father and children must realize that the children are not visitors in their father's house.

Whether you live in a house, an apartment, or only have a room somewhere, it is important that the children come to recognize your abode as a place where they can just *be* with you: play games, do homework, relax. If you can't provide a separate room for your visiting child, try to arrange some area that he knows is his, where he can leave toys or a book; provide some tie with you, some indication that he has a place in your home.

The Dependable Father

A father's dependability is of prime importance whether the child be toddler or teen-ager. Yet many a man, faced with the emotional tornadoes that can beset a part-time father, has found himself searching for a reasonable excuse to pass up a visiting day.

Eight-year-old Jonah was in such a bad mood last Sunday that nothing pleased him. Why go through another such performance? Certainly his monosyllabic phone conversation during the week didn't indicate that the sullen clouds had been dispersed. Yet this is the very moment that Jonah's

Daddy should be there. Whatever the cause for Jonah's unhappiness, whether he is angry with his father for what he interprets as desertion or unhappy because he is having a problem at school that he can't get himself to talk about, knowing that Daddy wants to be with him could help him over this hump.

Unless Daddy is a saint, he doesn't really want to be with Jonah when he's in a foul mood. Few of us willingly choose to inject ourselves into an unpleasant situation, but the divorced father can't expect he will be spared the black moods and emotional upsets he would have had to face had he been a full-time father.

Not all the unhappiness a child expresses is necessarily related to the situation of divorce. As every parent knows, life presents a child with many difficult situations—such as school or friendship—that he must master and conflicting feelings with which he must learn to cope.

As one father put it: "My visits with my children became less of a chore and more of a treat for me when I realized that the judge, in granting the divorce, hadn't granted my children the right to be treated any differently by me than when we all lived together. So now, when Pete goes into one of his occasional sulks, I no longer get tied up in knots. When I was living with the family, there were times when Pete wouldn't want to join us and would withdraw to his room. Then it seemed the natural thing to do was to let him know that while we wanted him with us, if he preferred not to join us, it was all right. After the divorce, when Pete repeated this behavior, I found myself tempted to buy his participation, to promise a new football, to offer a special treat. When I realized that I was being caught in the trap of offering 'things' because I felt guilty at having left Pete, sanity returned and I went back to treating him as I had before. I assured him that I wanted him with me, but if he preferred not to join me, that was his decision and I'd accept it, because I knew there would be other times when he would feel differently. Since I understand the situation better, I find I'm not running away from it (or even wanting to). In all honesty, I can't say I behave just as I did before the divorce. There's one big difference. If Pete is sulky or indifferent and it's my visiting day, I do make a special effort to see that he comes to my place. He can ignore me, read a book, watch TV, go into his room, but I always make it clear to him that I want him with me."

The Too-Literal Father

There are times when visitation assumes ludicrous forms. Because visitation rights are frequently so bitterly fought for, all too often there ensues a rigidity about living up to the letter of the law that has little bearing on the needs of the children involved. There are the young fathers who find themselves duty bound to spend the whole twenty-four hours assigned to them with their child. Richard P. would pick up eight-year-old Ted at nine o'clock on a Saturday morning armed with a fixed program: bicycle riding, lunch, movies, a walk to the nearest hamburger joint, and then "spending the evening together"—game after game of Monopoly or something similar. Richard never made any social engagements during his twenty-four hours with Ted. After several months of this routine, he became aware of his irritation with Ted, particularly when Ted seemed bored and not at all appreciative of the sacrifices his father was making for him.

At this point Richard began to take stock of what was happening. He realized that actually he and Ted were leading a very unnatural and stereotyped existence. Most fathers don't spend twenty-four hours a day exclusively and uninterruptedly with their children. Richard hadn't wanted to do it, but he thought Ted would feel he wasn't really sincere about wanting to be with him if he had arranged to be with friends and their children or if he had accepted an offer from Linda (his girl friend) to come over to his place and cook dinner for the three of them. Richard found that as he became more comfortable in his new relationship with Ted, he was able to approach their time together in a more relaxed fashion. His visits with Ted included a variety of experiences, some of which were exclusively with Ted and some of which included other people. This change gave Ted, living alone with his mother, an opportunity to observe how a man (Father) behaved not only with him but with others.

What about visits of the father who has remarried? (The subject of remarriage is more fully discussed in Chapter 9.) How does the introduction of a new person in the father's life affect the relationship of the part-time father and his children? Clark C. described his trials. "My boys were five, seven, and nine when Jean and I got married. I'd been divorced for a year, and when I knew that Jean and I were going to end up married (about three months before it actually came to pass), I had her meet the kids. They were a little wary of her at first, kind of holding back. She used to join us for dinner on my visiting days, and by the time we were married she and the boys were on great terms and I thought we were over the hump. Was I in for a surprise! We'd just gone off and been married quietly. The kids knew about it in advance, and for the first couple of weeks I thought things were going along well. Maybe I was just too happy with my own life to notice. But one Friday night when I called to speak to the boys, the two older ones, Tim and Frank, were in a great rush to get off the phone, and finally Tim blurted out, 'We can't come on Sunday. You can pick up Kevin.' And down went the receiver. I was stunned. I realized from the manner in which the message was relayed that something was very wrong. I waited a while and then called back and spoke to Tim, my nine-year-old. What came out reluctantly was that they had been trying to get up the courage to tell me they weren't enjoying the visits anymore since I'd gotten married. Jean was always there. Not that they didn't like her, but they felt they never had enough time to just be with me, the way they used to 'before you got Jean,' as Tim put it. Kevin didn't seem to mind, they said. We made a deal that they would come on Sunday and we would talk it over—without Jean. I thought about it a lot between that Friday and Sunday, and I could see where I'd gone off the track. I had misread their friendliness with Jean. Perhaps if they had openly resented her, I might not have been so insensitive to their feelings, but I was so happy with Jean that I guess I just wanted to believe everything else was falling neatly into place. As we talked together, the kids confirmed my feeling that while they liked Jean well enough, they resented having to share me with her on the one day a week they had with me. As a result we've changed things, and now the boys and I will spend the day together, and then Jean joins us for dinner. Or if we're visiting my parents, then I try to arrange that the boys and I are alone for lunch or dinner. It's not a hard and fast rule, and sometimes it doesn't work out, but I think what's emerged is a different focus in our time together. I try to have some time alone with the boys. I'd like to be able to spend time alone with each of them. Even before the divorce I always felt guilty about lumping them all together as 'the boys,' when they're such distinct individuals with different interests. Maybe now that they're getting older, I can arrange with Lois (my ex) to see them separately on an occasional Friday night."

Sometimes a remarried father may go off on visiting day and leave his daughter with his new wife, thinking it will give them a chance to get acquainted. Even though your daughter may like your new wife, it doesn't mean she wants to spend her visiting time with her. She wants to be with you. She doesn't need another mother; she needs her father. Unless she asks to spend time with your wife, she may well mis-understand your motives and feel rejected by your leaving her.

The Lonely Father

There are divorced fathers who feel lonely and deserted and use their visits with their children to hang onto the old relationship. They resent the separation from their family. They find their freedom a burden and live from visiting day to visiting day as a way of clinging to the old life.

George B. told us what such a man experiences. "Polly was twelve and Josh ten when I reluctantly accepted the fact that Joan was unshakable in her determination to end our fifteen-year marriage. It was a devastating experience for me. I couldn't believe Joan's protestations that there wasn't anybody else in her life, but that what had been between us was over. I'm not pretending I ever got over that, but I finally consoled myself that I still had my relationship with my kids, which had always been a good one. I got an apartment with an extra bedroom and a convertible couch in the living room in one of those new buildings with a swimming pool, so that the kids could stay over with me. I began to anticipate the good times we were going to have each weekend. The kids and I always loved swimming, and coming to the city from the suburbs would be a nice change for them. As happy as I had been with Joan, I saw her faults, and I began to think that maybe this divorce might have some positive aspects for the kids, get them out from under some of her compulsive, driving pressures. Things went along well at first. The weekends were the center of my life; and since I was used to spending a lot of time with the kids, it all seemed very natural. I just didn't feel up to 'making a new life for myself.' Once in a while I'd call the kids during the week, thinking I might drive up and take them out to dinner, but they seemed always to be busy with music lessons, dancing lessons, and all those other damned things Joan arranged for them, so that it never worked out. I always felt down in the dumps after something like this fell through and was more impatient than ever for the weekend.

"After a few months I began to get that same depressed feeling when the weekend was over. Something was missing. Then one day Polly called to say she couldn't come in with Josh on Saturday because a boy had asked her to a party, but she'd meet us on Sunday. I was so disappointed I couldn't even hear the excitement in her voice that the 'right boy' had asked her. I didn't make any effort to hide my disappointment. I snapped at Polly that since we had tickets for a football game for Sunday (which I thought she was eager to go to), she probably wouldn't be able to get into town early enough for that so she might as well skip coming in this weekend altogether. To my dismay she was delighted. Betsy, her best friend, was going to the party and wanted her to sleep over afterward. She'd see me the following weekend. 'OK,' I said grudgingly, and hung up. I was pretty miserable all weekend and found myself asking Josh about his mother—all those questions that plagued me as I sat home alone all week. Who was she seeing? Where was she this weekend? I didn't realize at the time that Josh evaded answering my questions. The following weekend Polly came in with Josh. I had been looking forward to the visit all week, yet after the weekend I felt miserable and depressed. This went on for a couple of months. Then one weekend, just after we'd come up from the pool, Polly exploded: 'Can't you stop bugging us with all your questions about Mommy? Don't you see what a rotten spot you put us in? We don't like being stoolies.' Then it all poured out—how they felt that I was only interested in seeing them in order to find out about their mother. Polly added her own gripe; I had never even asked her if she had had a good time at the party. I wish I could say that this outburst cleared the air. It didn't. I was miserable and acted miserably. I told the kids that if this was the way they felt, maybe we should cool it and skip the next visit. I drove them to the train in silence and left them abruptly. I was utterly dejected all week. I couldn't keep my mind on my work; my desk was piling up. I was snapping at everyone until Bart, a colleague and good friend of mine, came in and wanted to know what the trouble was. I started to pour out my woes. Bart let me go on for a while, then said that he thought I ought to talk to a professional person who could be more helpful. I felt he was letting me down, but I was so unhappy that in desperation I accepted his suggestion.

"This was the turning point in my adjustment to the

divorce, and I feel that it saved my relationship with my children. It didn't happen overnight. I began to see how I had been trying to use my kids, particularly Polly, as a balm for the wounds that Joan had inflicted, and to understand that I had reacted to Polly's perfectly normal excitement over her first dance as a repetition of Joan's rejection. I'm a lucky guy that I had a backlog of all those good years with my kids, so that they were able to tell me off. I knew that I had never really accepted the divorce, but what I hadn't realized was how I had been using my kids to keep my ties to Joan alive."

George is not the only divorced father who has exploited his children for his own needs. There are many variations on this theme. Children of divorce are often used as footballs in the game played by their parents, who allow the anger and resentment against their ex-mates to affect their relationship with their children. This anger can be expressed in an infinite variety of subtle ways. There is the father who won't change a visiting day so that his children can go on a picnic with their mother and her boy friend, or the father who is critical of the way his children are dressed or is openly derogatory about their mother. Children caught in this bind realize very quickly that their father's first priority is not so much concern for them as it is a need to use them as a conduit for his negative feelings toward their mother, and they may invent excuses to avoid seeing him. Since such a father is often quite unaware of the message he is transmitting by his behavior, he is puzzled at his children's response. If you find your children are reluctant to see you and if they can't or won't tell you what is bothering them, you may get some clues by examining your own behavior.

Then there is the father who is casual about visiting; who arrives late to pick up the children or says he'll have them back at six and returns them at nine. You may have been vaguely aware of their mother's anger at these times but dismissed it as just part of her rigidity—one of the things you were never able to abide in her. She may well be rigid, but chances are that she probably arranged her own plans so that she would be home when the children got back. Your casualness about time can be hard on the children, too, because they have to face her anger when you bring them home late. Next time they may invent excuses to avoid seeing you because of their fear of her wrath.

If, for whatever the reason, your children won't see you, let them know that you are available whenever they change their minds. Naturally, you may feel hurt or rejected. But remember, you are the adult. It is up to you to take the initiative in making contact with them; always keep some line of communication open. You can do this by remembering a birthday or a holiday, or just dropping a note to let your children know you're thinking of them.

Just Like Her Mother

Many an anguished father has asked, "What am I to do when I see my children duplicating the very behavior and values that I can't bear in their mother? All she is concerned about is getting 'things.'" Certainly, two people who admire and respect each other generally aren't the ones who get divorced. But criticizing your children's mother or launching into moralistic lectures on values may adversely affect children who are living in a world of divided loyalties. Your attacks may make them feel they have to defend their mother, and they may end up being ill at ease with you. Some of your children's traits may upset you because they indeed inject their mother's presence into your visits and spoil your time together. But try to understand their behavior. Children who have the "gimmes" are not necessarily duplicates of their materialistic mother. They may be seeking reassurance of their father's love in terms they know best—being given presents.

How Much Do You Love Me?

Akin to this behavior is a child's attempt to test the father's interest. Seth said he couldn't possibly see his father on Saturday because he had to go to the school library and that would mean a long subway ride, but if Dad wanted to pick him up and take him to the library that would be OK. Since Seth made that subway ride five days a week, his father was able to interpret the message: Do you care enough about seeing me to go out of your way for me? The best reassurance a child can get is not from Father's meeting his every request but from the consistency and reliability of his father's relationship with him.

The Man-About-Town

The man who often has the most difficult time in adjusting to his visitation privileges is the one most delighted to be freed from the bonds of matrimony. He is pleased with his bachelor existence and often is on the run from one entanglement to another. He really wants to see his children and does, erratically and often inappropriately. He remembers that it's his visiting day, but his luncheon date lasted longer than he expected, he explains to his disappointed children when he calls at five o'clock. A few days later he may call at eight. He's in the neighborhood; why don't the children come out to dinner with him and some friends? Needless to say, the children have already had dinner. And so it goes.

A party, a weekend invitation, these take priority over his arrangements with his children. He may try to effect a compromise and take his children with him on his dates. The children may find this exciting, but more often they feel uncomfortable, knowing they will have to face their mother's criticism of their father when they get home.

Or he may try to have his cake and eat it, too, by keeping his date and dumping his children on his parents or another available relative. Children need a relationship with grandparents and other relatives, but not in place of one with their father. Rather than including the children inappropriately or making last-minute cancellations, it might be better if such a father arranged a schedule that was more in accord with his life style. Even an hour a week that the children can count on is far better for both children and father than the bitterness of the children's disappointment and feeling of betrayal when Father doesn't show up.

Visiting with Children and Their Friends

As time goes on and the children feel more reassured that they haven't been abandoned, the relationship between part-time father and children becomes more relaxed. When this happens, the child who in the early postdivorce period was tentative about revealing anything personal will want to share with his father not only his interests but his friends. Some fathers don't like this. They consider it an intrusion upon their limited visiting time; they feel that the child is in some way trying to protect himself against any closeness. Unless the demand to include friends is excessive, a father may well feel pleased with himself for succeeding in solidifying the relationship.

Visiting and the Adolescent

As your children enter adolescence, be prepared for changes in the nature of the visits—and for disappointments.

Your daughter likes the idea of getting away from Mother and spending the weekend at your place. You are delighted. You prepare dinner and eagerly await her arrival. She is charming and helpful and you enjoy dinner together. As you're finishing dessert, the door bell rings. She exclaims, as though it's a surprise to her, "That must be Jeff, he's taking me to the Rolling Stones concert. Don't wait up for me," she chirps sweetly, "I may be quite late." Before you know it, she's out the door.

The adolescent may well use your place as a kind of hotel, a stopover place to sleep, take a bath, and grab a bite between dashings around town. At the close of the weekend you find that you have had time for little more than a few perfunctory words with him or her—that and cleaning up the mess afterward. You may be hurt or angry as well as disappointed, feeling that you were being used. Had you been living at home with your child, seeing him daily, you would have shrugged off such behavior as standard operating procedure for an adolescent. As a part-time father it is understandable that you feel cheated. You will have to reconcile yourself to the self-centeredness of adolescence. Instead of being hurt, console yourself with the fact that your child feels comfortable enough with you to treat you as you are—the father of an adolescent.

Slipups and misunderstandings about appointment time and place are legion and make for an angry or disappointed father. Adolescents are hardly noted for getting places on schedule. Fathers complain that their teen-agers don't meet them on time or sometimes not at all. Or just when a father is all set to have a heart-to-heart talk with his son, the boy shows up with a friend or two, ruling out any chance of intimacy.

Fathers tell us the story again and again. They are all prepared to have a good time with their children. They promise themselves not to get upset about anything the children say or do—just enjoy being together. They await the children's arrival eagerly. With each passing moment that the children are late, the good feelings are gradually dissipated. By the time they show up, if they show up at all, the father is so upset and angry that the meeting starts off on the left foot.

Here is the experience of Andrew L.: "I was waiting for Steve and Ben to show up at my apartment. (Steve is fourteen, Ben sixteen.) I was thinking how nice it would be if I'd spend a week or two with the boys next summer camping out in the Canadian Rockies, hiking in the woods, fishing for trout in a stream I used to fish with my own father, sharing with them some of the marvelous experiences I had as a boy. I tell you, it was a beautiful daydream.

"So what happens? Nobody shows up. Finally, about two hours late, Steve appears. I ask him, Where's Ben? He says he doesn't know; Ben never came home last night. Fine business. What the hell kind of mother have they got, that a sixteen-year-old kid wet behind the ears stays out all night?

"And you should have seen Steve. He looked like some goddam faggot with his long hair tied back with a ribbon—a ribbon! He was wearing a flowered shirt and a kind of necklace he called an amulet. All my resolutions to have a good visit, to talk about next summer, not to argue or criticize—all flew out the window. First thing you know I'm yelling at him for keeping me waiting and for looking like a creep and how I'm ashamed to go out with him. He gets sore and yells back, and the next thing you know he slams the door and is gone. I felt so bad I had to take a drink, and then another and another. Well, I don't have to tell you how that day ended up."

Visiting on Special Occasions

If your son or daughter goes to a school or camp that has a special visiting day for parents, he or she may not want you and Mother to visit at the same time. Respect your children's wishes. Most schools and camps are well acquainted with these situations and are able to make the necessary arrangements for alternate visiting. On the other hand, your children may insist that both parents come together because they have not been able to accept the reality of the divorce and cannot see their parents as separate people. Though you may want to please them, going along with this request will not be of any help to them.

Being a visiting father is not easy. It takes love, interest, understanding, and, most of all, patience. Eventually you will find that the time spent with your children, which originally seemed so artificial and uncomfortable, has now become an enjoyable and accepted part of your new life.

7
MONEY, MONEY, MONEY

There is something about money—wanting it, getting it, giving it—that brings out the worst in people. Money is far more than Mr. Webster's definition: ". . . a medium of exchange, a measure of value, or a means of payment. . . ." Money has many hidden emotional meanings. It symbolizes different things to different people. For most people, rich and poor alike, money is a symbol of status, influence, authority. For some people money represents love. Or it serves as a substitute for love. For others it means security—not just economic security but emotional security. To pathological hoarders, hanging on to money or possessions is like hanging on to life itself. It is not uncommon to read newspaper stories of people, found dead of starvation, in whose hovels thousands of dollars were discovered. To say that these persons hoarded money for fear of impoverishment ignores the profound emotional significance of money in people's lives.

Money as Scapegoat

In times of emotional stress, unconscious attitudes and feelings ordinarily kept buried break through and color our behavior. At such times our feelings about money become irrational. Instead of being an objective commodity, it becomes a scapegoat for unspoken needs. Even in so-called intact marriages, surveys have shown that arguments over money are one of the most frequent causes of marital discord. The real sore spot may not be money at all, though on the surface it may look like it to both husband and wife. For example, a wife complains that her husband doesn't give her enough money to run the house; the husband retorts that she doesn't know how to handle money. The man may indeed be stingy and the woman extravagant. But underneath their complaints may lurk the real mainspring of their conflict—in this case it may be a struggle for dominance, or sexual dissatisfaction, or other unspoken needs. Here money becomes the standard-bearer in the battle between them.

In marriages where love has gone, money is not uncommonly used as a device for reward or punishment—given or withheld, for example, as a quid pro quo for sexual relations. The use of money as expiation for guilt is commonplace. Buying the wife a gift as atonement for sexual dalliance outside the marriage bed is a banality scarcely worth mentioning. Conversely, there is hardly a woman who has not at one time or another made some extravagant expenditure on herself or her home out of unspoken anger or in unconscious revenge against an unsuspecting husband for an injury, real or imagined, to her self-esteem. One woman we know "accidentally" loses large sums of money when she feels irrationally jealous of her husband.

Money as Weapon

It is especially during the breaking-up and early separation period, when emotional turmoil is at its height, that the dark side of one's character, ordinarily kept hidden from oneself as well as others, comes to the fore. One becomes stingy, greedy, or mean-souled. Money—its retention or expenditure —becomes the handiest tool for striking at the "enemy."

During that gray, in-between period of separation when the man is still legally responsible for his wife's debts, one woman may buy herself a fur coat her husband can ill afford. Another may redecorate the apartment. Still another may empty out the joint bank account. A man may summarily cut off his wife's charge accounts or dole out a niggardly allowance. Another may send his wife no money at all when she takes the children and leaves home. At the bargaining table, the thrifty, penny-pinching housewife may make financial demands beyond all reason. The open-handed husband may try to hide his financial assets and shell out as little as he can get away with.

In separation and divorce, where the real coin of the realm is anger, pain, vengefulness and hate, money serves as the symbol for everything that went wrong with the marriage. It becomes the socially sanctioned weapon with which each adversary tries to beat down his opponent. It can be wielded mercilessly with relentless fury in moral righteousness, with no shred of guilt.

More often than not, the children, in whose cause these bitter battles presumably rage, are all but forgotten. In many a harsh custody fight, judges tell us, the force driving each contender is not so much concern for the best interests of the children as for the money involved in their support. In such cases, behind the father's battle for custody lies the determination that "I'm not going to give that harridan one cent"; behind the mother's, "That bastard's going to pay plenty for what he's done." Used as a pawn to best the opponent, the children are the ultimate victims of the fray.

Dividing the Kitty

Like death and taxes, one thing is certain in separation and divorce: except for the very rich, *there is never enough money.*

In theory the amount of money to be allotted for the support of the ex-wife and children should be decided on realistic considerations: How much money does the father—and mother, if she works—earn? How much will the separate households need? How can the two facts be best reconciled? In practice, nobody is satisfied. Each side feels shortchanged.

Except for the very rich, supporting two households on the same amount of money that formerly supported one means an undeniable fact—a lower standard of living for each. No one wants to accept this harsh reality. To the woman whose husband wanted the divorce, it adds insult to injury. It means having to make do with less money on top of losing the man of the house. To the man whose wife wanted out, it means having to cope not only with grief, loneliness, and discontinuance of a way of life but with less money for himself, sometimes barely enough for his basic physical needs. When we think of the emotional significance of money—its giving and getting—the additional deprivation of material comforts at a time of greatest emotional vulnerability is salt in one's wounds.

Alimony

Every decent father wants to have his children properly cared for and is willing, to the extent he is able, to provide for that care in the custody of the mother. The bone in the throat is alimony. To divorced men, paying alimony, as one TV comic crudely puts it, "is like buying oats to feed a dead horse." Some men are vociferously opposed to alimony. Charles V. Metz, in his book *Divorce and Custody for Men,* in a chapter entitled "Alimony, the Shameful Vice," writes: "Of all the sadistic shackles that modern, freed, equalized woman has placed upon men, alimony is the worst. Because alimony can never pay for services rendered, and because alimony invariably results in mutual hatred, it should be abolished altogether. No thinking moral man should respect any woman who accepts it. No thinking moral man should ever forgive any man who pays it willingly."

In an adversary system of divorce (which stems from archaic ecclesiastical laws) under which most states operate, one spouse is declared "guilty," the other "innocent," even though, as judge, attorneys, plaintiff, defendant, and witnesses know, both parties in most divorces have come to an agreement as to which shall be which (as well as an agreement on property settlement, custody, support, and visitation) before the case reaches the court. Nonetheless, under such an adversary system the woman, usually declared the "innocent" party by mutual consent and regarded under the law as helpless and dependent on the man for support, is entitled to alimony.

If a woman is too old or incapacitated to work at the time of divorce and other financial resources are unavailable to her, permanent alimony would be justified. But in the case of the average divorcée (the average age is 31.7 years), alimony should be *temporary*—paid only until the children are old enough to go to nursery or elementary school and the mother, if she has no marketabe skills, has time to be trained for gainful employment.

Paying alimony incites a man's meanest feelings—hatred, resentment, impotent rage. He regards it as unfair punishment for a youthful error in judgment or for an unsought change in feelings that rendered the marriage untenable. "Paying alimony," writes Joseph Epstein in *Divorced in America*, ". . . becomes a condition of one's existence, something that must be taken into consideration with every move one makes, a burden one must drag through life, like a club foot. [Alimony] . . . can be a life-stretch—with no time off for good behavior. . . . A harsh sentence for a man whose only error may have been marrying the wrong woman."

Putting a woman on a permanent dole can be destructive, even debasing for her. She justifies taking permanent alimony as "retribution from a defeated enemy . . . a lifetime pension for injuries sustained in marital combat," says Bernard

Steinzor in *When Parents Divorce.* Vengeance or the dubious pleasures of self-pity and martyrdom have turned many a woman who might have become an independent, socially productive human being into a parasite, a social cripple.

Alimony can also be a source of shame to children, particularly adolescents, if they see it as an instrument of exploitation of the father. Not infrequently, a woman will refrain from marrying a man with whom she is living in order to continue to collect alimony. Such an arrangement puts children in an awkward position vis-à-vis their father. Luke, twelve, started to avoid seeing his father with rather flimsy excuses. It turned out that he did not want to reveal to his father that the mother's boy friend had moved into their home. Yet keeping this secret from the father made him uncomfortable; so he resolved his dilemma by avoiding contact with his father altogether. Mary, sixteen, wept as she reported that her mother had taken her unemployed boy friend to Europe on "my Daddy's money."

One may ask: Why do men consent to the payment of alimony? For one, a man will consent to anything if he wants to get out of the marriage badly enough (sometimes, out of guilt, paying more than he can afford). For another, the wife's lawyer may insist on it as an inflexible condition of divorce, especially if the property settlement is small; for while child support ceases when the children are grown, alimony continues forever if the ex-wife does not remarry. Moreover, for tax purposes—and in many cases it is the primary reason—the man's lawyer will advise his client to stipulate in the divorce contract a specific amount for alimony and a separate specified amount for child support, since alimony is tax deductible whereas child support is not.

Some states have abolished the adversary system and in its stead have instituted what is called no-fault divorce in which the sole basis for divorce is the irremediable breakdown of the marriage. In other words, if one partner no longer wants to continue the relationship—thereby making family life an impossibility—the marriage ceases to exist. Under no-fault divorce, property acquired during the marriage is divided equally between husband and wife. No alimony is awarded the woman, except for a specified period of time agreed upon that may be necessary to help her adjust to the changed family situation and to prepare her for self-support.

However, child support under no-fault divorce includes support for the mother for as long as she is the children's caretaker. For a woman who is physically strong and of average intelligence, to depend on support payments for her children—unless they are young enough to need her full-time care—as a means of livelihood for herself, is demeaning. The women's liberation movement has performed a great service to women—and men, too—in helping women become more aware of their potential capacities not only as mothers and wives but as socially, politically, and economically productive human beings outside the home. The time may come in the not-too-distant future when the mother, insofar as her circumstances permit, will feel as responsible for the support of the children as the father.

Child Support

Civilized man—and probably prehistoric man as well—has always assumed the role of provider for his family. Most separated or divorced fathers willingly assume the responsibility of providing for their children insofar as they are able. Of course, there will be a clash of economic interests and differences of opinion between the embattled adversaries as to what constitutes "able." Parents will disagree about what proportion of the father's earnings should go for the children's support. The mother may insist that the children should continue to live at the same standard as if there had been no divorce. Why should they be penalized for the parents' mistakes? she demands. Father objects. It's impossible if he is to live decently. Why should he continue supporting them if he has nothing left for himself? Neurotic hang-ups about money as well as the hard reality of its short supply can keep this battle going for a long, long time.

Support versus Visitation

In most divorce contracts, stipulations regarding support and visiting rights are spelled out separately. That is, the father agrees to certain financial responsibilities toward the children, and he is also given certain rights in regard to visiting with them. The two are mutually exclusive. (In rare contracts the two are interlocked.)

Visiting rights are not established in exchange for support. Yet in the mind not only of the mother but also of the father, the contract is often so interpreted. Power over the use of visiting rights is one of the few weapons the mother has at her disposal as custodial parent. If the father does not fully meet his contractual responsibilities or if the ex-wife is still looking for ways to punish him, what better way than to prevent or hamper his seeing the children? If he falls behind in his support payments, he can be and often is refused the right to see his children. As one father bitterly expressed it "No checkee, no washee."

Children as Losers

The children are inevitably the losers. Philip Z. loses his job and falls behind in his support payments. Ruth Z., helpless in this situation, in her anger and desperation at being deprived of the needed support, threatens that if he doesn't bring the money, she won't let him see the children. Much as he wants to see them, he feels he isn't entitled to the privilege since he isn't supporting them now. Moreover, he is ashamed and doesn't want to be confronted with his inadequacy by his ex-wife when he calls for them. So he fails to show up on the day the kids expect him. It would take a very mature and understanding woman to refrain from pointing out to the children not only the father's failure to provide but his seeming lack of interest in them.

Children of divorce can lose in other ways. A not uncommon story: Ethel R. remarries and takes the two children to live with her new husband halfway across the continent. Norman R. is angry at his ex-wife for taking the children so far away that he can scarcely afford to visit them once a year. (He may also be unconsciously angry at her for finding a new mate, for being happy while he's still miserable.) For a while he continues to send money for child support regularly. Eventually he remarries. Money gets tight. Guiltily he cuts the allowance. One child, two children arrive. Money gets tighter. More guiltily, he misses payments. His second wife resents having to pinch and scrape so that he can send money to kids he hardly ever hears from. Resentments pile up. Why should I deprive my family for kids who don't even care if I'm alive? He still can't stomach the idea of another man supporting them, though he hears that her second husband is doing very well in business. Maybe the support money he can barely scrape together is just "chicken feed" to her. He writes to his children occasionally, sends them cards on their birthdays. They seldom write back. Finally letters stop altogether. So do his checks. The children gradually fade out of his life. He recalls them only as little ones, although his mind tells him they must be in high school by now. One day he gets a letter from his former wife asking if he will release the children for adoption by their stepfather. They want to take his name. Norman is stunned. Everyone is the loser, especially the children. By default.

In the hassle over money children are used as barter more often than we care to admit.

Take the C.'s. In the divorce contract, Joel C., an attorney, was given the right to have Betsy, age five, for the summer vacation. There was no specific stipulation in the decree about child support during the time the child would be with him. The father, remarried and with a new baby, had taken a cottage at the seashore for the family and wanted Betsy with them for the summer. Since he would be taking full charge of the child for the ten weeks she would be with him, he felt he shouldn't have to pay the mother full child support for that period. Mother, on the other hand, insisted on full payment, since certain expenses like rent, telephone, and utilities went on whether the child was home or not. After much dickering, the father offered to pay one half, though he considered it a holdup. The mother held out for the full amount. Each was adamant. It ended up by Betsy remaining with her mother in the city. The father was deprived of the pleasure of Betsy's company that summer, and the mother was deprived of a vacation without the child. Both parents felt justified in their stance, though both were losers in this power struggle. But it was Betsy who was the real victim of this Pyrrhic victory.

A more friendly way, of benefit to the entire family, is that of the O's. The father, a schoolteacher (who earns less than Joel C.) lives hundreds of miles away from his three children, ages six, nine, and eleven, and can see them only on holidays. Every summer he takes them camping in Maine. He gives the support money for that period to the mother, who uses it to travel. They all have a fine holiday. Such an amicable arrangement bespeaks real emotional freedom from the ties of anger, hate, and resentment that bind so many ex-mates together.

Sometimes a father, whether through guilt, or to demonstrate his love in a concrete way, or to counteract the mother's disparagement of him and show the children he is really a good guy, will spend prodigally on his children even at the cost of depriving himself of necessities.

Daniel M. was such a father. A government clerk of modest means, on his weekly visits he would take his two children, eight and ten, to expensive restaurants (they would have preferred franks at the deli), movies, ballgames, or other commercial entertainment and load them with toys beyond their needs, though this meant his forgoing proper lunches. Instead of serving the children as a *father,* he had turned himself into a bountiful uncle or doting grandpa. Moreover, the children's sense of economic reality became distorted. Their mother's necessary penny-pinching as contrasted with their father's free-and-easy spending on them was at the very least confusing. It bred complaints against the mother for denial of requests for "things" and retaliation against her by getting them from the father. In this case Daniel's need to buy his children's love through overindulgence was detrimental not only to their relationship to their mother but to their healthy development as well.

Where the Money Goes

How the support money is used is another sore spot in the battle between ex-spouses. In this battle, the custodial parent always wins and the children are the spoils of war. Even in compatible marriages husbands and wives often have quite different ideas about what each considers a necessity or a luxury. These differences become sharpened in divorce. It is a rare man who does not resent the fact that he has no say over how "his" money is being spent by the ex-wife. He may be doling out barely enough to feed and clothe the children. Nonetheless, he feels it a rank injustice that he must stand helplessly by, his hands tied by legal decree, while she "squanders" his hard-earned money on what he considers frivolities and nonessentials. In families where the man had managed the finances, paid the bills, and given the wife money only as needed to pay for groceries, it does sometimes happen after the divorce that the woman, upon taking charge of handling the finances for herself and the children, does it poorly, at least at the beginning of her stewardship. Complaints of ex-wives' foolish extravagances for the children while shortchanging them on proper food or clothing are common. (In some separation or divorce contracts, the father stipulates certain specific large expenses he will be responsible for, such as insurance, medical and dental care, and higher education.) Every divorced father has his own horror tale to recount.

How one spends money is an individual matter. What is one person's extravagance is another person's necessity. How the custodial parent handles the support money cannot be legislated, even by the divorced father who provides it. If discussion with the ex-spouse leads nowhere but to further argument and recriminations, the best you can do is to settle for a philosophical attitude. "What can I do," Warren M. asks in helpless rage, "when Rose is always spending my money on some cockamamie junk and then running short?"

You can't do much, Warren M. This is the price you pay for being released from a hopeless marriage.

What Every Child (of Divorce) Should Know

It is surprising how seldom children are told by either parent about the arrangements for their support. They know in a general way that Daddy sends Mommy money—heaven knows they hear enough talk about it—but we have found in our work with children of divorce that even older children are often kept (or keep themselves) in the dark about money matters. Perhaps, because the matter is so emotionally charged, parents find it a painful subject to discuss with their children and settle for vague, sometimes veiled, hints that leave the children with distorted notions. Children hear enough disparaging innuendoes from their separated parents about the ex-spouse—how "tight" the father, how extravagant the mother—to feel queasy about bringing up the subject, so a conspiracy of silence prevails about the very issue they are most concerned with.

Like the matter of the separation itself, how much they

are told about the financial agreement will depend on their age and level of understanding. Father may not bother to spell out for the children something he takes for granted: that he will be responsible for the support of the family even though he no longer lives under the same roof. Yet to the children it is very important that they hear this assurance in concrete words. Without them, children, especially young ones, feeling abandoned and unprotected, can weave all kinds of frightening fantasies.

The older child should be told specifically what the father is providing. This is especially important if the family's standard of living is lowered—as it usually is—because of the cost of two households instead of one. The child may have to transfer from private to public school, move to a smaller house, give up piano lessons, or spend his vacation at Uncle Milt's farm instead of in a rented cottage at the beach. He can accept this disappointment with better grace if he knows the family's economic "facts of life" than if he is left to his fantasies about the deprivation. He may not like it. He may be angry about it and kick up a storm; but it won't be because he thinks you don't care for him anymore.

Knowing the economic facts can help an adolescent in his growth toward maturity. Many a young person has gotten himself a job to earn spending money or even to contribute toward the household expenses. Pitching in to help the family or to support oneself, at least in part, can be a gratifying experience and a source of pride to a young person growing up in an uncertain world.

Knowing the economic facts can help an adolescent's emotional development in other ways. Allen, seventeen, a timid boy, was living with his mother while attending a community college. His divorced father, an authoritarian figure, agreed to pay his tuition and other expenses connected with his education, such as books and lab fees, in addition to the monthly allowance to the mother for the boy's support. In his visits with Allen, Father learned that the boy carried his lunch to school, attended few college events, participated in no extracurricular activities, and seldom dated a girl. He learned further that the mother was doling out two dollars a day to the boy, hardly enough to cover his transportation costs.

Having no spending money prevented Allen from participating in school events. The exact amount of the father's payment for his support and what it was meant to cover had never been discussed with him. Mother had so impressed him with their poverty and with his father's stinginess that the boy was reluctant to complain to either parent about his chronic lack of funds.

Father was so outraged by what he considered the mother's callousness toward the boy's social needs that he high-handedly decided to give the support money directly to Allen, who would in turn pay his mother. But the boy was too frightened to assume such an adult responsibility. Realizing, however, he was far from a "welfare" case, he was able to ask his mother for an increased allowance. Now he could join his peers. Thus he was able to get going on the road toward freeing himself from his infantilizing mother and his powerful father.

Raising the Ante

In many divorce situations, the mother tries to add fringe benefits to the original agreement by using a variety of devices. Eric, nine, shows up for his visit with Dad wearing torn sneakers and jeans he has clearly outgrown. When Dad questions him about this, Eric mumbles in a small doleful voice that Mother says they have no money for shoes or new pants. Father rants against the boy's mother. He gives her enough to dress his kids properly; what the hell does she do with his money? He may then buy Eric new shoes and pants, but grudgingly, not only because it means depriving himself of some necessity but because he feels himself exploited. Or he may stand on his "rights"—the support allowance includes the cost of clothing, she should buy it!—and send the boy back as he came. In either case Eric is made to feel bad—a football in the eternal scrimmage between his divorced parents.

Another device is to send the children to visit the paternal grandparents or other relatives looking, as one father described them, "like orphans of the storm." The expectation, whether conscious or unconscious, is to make relatives bring pressure to bear upon the "selfish" father to do better by his children or, at the very least, to exhibit to the relatives how callous or uncaring their son (or brother or nephew) is. Children are extremely sensitive to such maneuvers. They may resent being exploited as objects of pity and refuse to visit the relatives. Or, as frequently happens, they may fall in with the mother's need to put their father in a bad light and take on the stance of the stereotyped "poor orphans."

A father we know who has a splendid relationship with his six-year-old daughter noticed that when he praised a new dress or coat she was wearing, she was quick to say, "Mommy didn't buy it; Grandma gave it to me," or, "Aunt Laura made it for me." An open, bubbly, confiding child, she would sometimes become silent or laconic when her father asked her, out of sheer interest, what she did last weekend. (He lived in another city and saw her only every other weekend.) He eventually deduced that she would clam up if she had enjoyed some entertainment or gone on some excursion with her mother that cost money. She was privy to the telephone battles between her parents that always centered around money, and she quickly picked up the nonverbal cue that she should avoid conversation about things that involved the expenditure of money. In her need to protect her mother, her beloved father became an "alien enemy" to be guarded against in this emotionally charged arena. (One speculates on how this experience may eventually condition her feelings about money vis-à-vis men in her adulthood.)

Rich Man, Poor Man

We don't know whether children of separation and divorce are more preoccupied with possessions and money matters than children of intact marriages. From our experience it would seem so. We have been struck by how much of their talk, especially of those youngsters about ten or older, centers on "things"—the getting or not getting of them—and their feelings about them.

The division of property and other money matters is a hot, if not the hottest, issue in divorce, and fights over it are seldom kept secret from the children. For those children whose separated and divorced parents use the unending money battle to hang on neurotically to the old relationship, material possessions—or the lack of them—can become an abiding preoccupation. We know that to a young child, being given concrete "things" can mean love. "Daddy gives me presents. He still loves me," thinks the four-year-old. It can also represent to a child a measure of his worth. "Whee! Daddy gave me a bike! Last year he said I was too young. He trusts me now to be careful and take good care of it."

A child tends to incorporate within himself parental values, which include the attitude toward possessions. If conspicuous consumption is an important aspect of the parents' way of life, chances are that the display of material things as a symbol of success will be important to their offspring.

(The reverse is also true. Some adolescents, in their need to free themselves from dependence on their parents, will cast off their parents' values and live in a manner quite opposite to that in which they were reared: the middle-class adolescent from suburbia who moves to a pad in the slums, the son of a radical political leader who becomes a stockbroker.)

Among the traumas that children of divorce are vulnerable to, overconcern with money matters is one of the most insidious. They are especially sensitive to differences in the standards of living of the parents, particularly if one (or both) is remarried. They compare the living quarters, the make of car, even the food served, and are pained by evidence that one is better off than the other.

Sometimes a parent, meaning no harm, will play on the differences, stirring up in the child a disturbing conflict of loyalties. Marion comes home after a visit with Father and his second wife and enthusiastically describes the lobster dinner they shared at a fancy seafood restaurant. Mother sighs as she serves the frankfurters and beans for supper and murmurs that she hasn't been in a restaurant for months. Marion feels guilty for having had a good time with Father.

Dad wears the same shabby slacks and sweater whenever the kids visit him. He can't afford new clothes because "all my money goes to your mother." They see Mother all dressed up to go out on a date, and instead of taking pleasure in her attractiveness they find themselves resentful over "what she's done to Dad"—a common reaction of adolescent girls.

Sometimes, because of circumstances, the parents live at very disparate economic levels. This can be quite upsetting to a child. Paul was a victim of such a situation.

Paul, age seven, lived with his divorced mother in a cramped city apartment, supported modestly by his father's monthly allowance and his mother's earnings as a part-time salesperson in a department store. Pennies had to be counted. About a year after the divorce, Father, an advertising man, married a wealthy widow with two children, a girl of fifteen and a boy Paul's age. He moved into his wife's elegant home in a suburb on a large estate equipped with swimming pool, tennis court, game room.

Paul, who had maintained a close relationship with his father throughout the separation and divorce, was now spending weekends in his father's new residence. Father was happy that he could give his son the advantages of the good life his remarriage had made possible. Not long afterward, Paul, who had weathered the breakup of his family without apparent trauma, began to develop symptoms for which no physical basis could be found—headaches, allergies, and gastrointestinal and other random pains. His schoolwork fell off; he cried easily; he began to stay in the house because he thought the kids in the neighborhood didn't like him. His mother thought he was depressed because he missed his father, who had gone to Europe for a vacation with his second family.

When Paul finally refused to leave the house even to go to school, he was referred for therapy. It turned out that no one had thought to explain to the boy that it was his father's rich second wife who was responsible for keeping her children in the style to which they had been accustomed. Paul had assumed that it was his father who was providing so lavishly for his stepchildren, a sure sign that he preferred *them* to *him.* Nothing could easily assuage Paul's resentment of his stepsiblings, who not only had so many possessions but also his father's daily companionship. But knowing the facts did make him feel less discriminated against and no longer so angry.

Haggling Can Help

Ugly, painful, sickening as the haggling over money and property in the process of divorce may be, it serves an important and useful purpose—to de-value the former spouse. In the course of a deteriorating marriage, not only does hate replace love, but disenchantment becomes an essential ingredient of emotional disengagement. For a time it is easier—and necessary—to see the "ex" as a "stingy bastard" or "a money-mad bloodsucker" than to see the person whole. Only when the haggling finally stops—perhaps years after the legal procedures have been over—does a divorce become real.

When Ralph, now twenty-eight, was divorced six years ago from Irene after three years of a disastrous "forced" marriage, an "escalator clause" in the decree provided that any increase in his salary was to be followed by a proportionate increase in the alimony and support payments for his child Debbie, then two and a half. The payments were small, since at the time of divorce Ralph was earning a modest salary as a bank clerk in training for an eventual managerial position, and it seemed only fair that as his fortunes rose he should provide more amply for his child and ex-wife. However, he remarried after a year and the following year his wife had a baby, and whatever raises in pay he received barely covered the extra expenses of his second family. An increase in support payments was out of the question at the time.

Although at the beginning he rarely saw Debbie (she lived with her mother in another town), after his remarriage Ralph resumed his relationship with her, taking her to his home for weekends, holidays, and vacations. His wife Doris, a mature, understanding young woman, was able to control whatever jealousy she felt toward this reminder of Ralph's first wife and was a good and loving stepmother to Debbie during her visits.

What bothered Doris, however, were the interminable long-distance calls from Irene to Ralph (and from Ralph to Irene) ostensibly about arrangements for picking up Debbie and returning her, what she shouldn't do, shouldn't wear, shouldn't eat—the child had a collection of allergies—ending inevitably with demands from Irene for more money. Ralph would hang up after these long, haranguing calls a "nervous wreck," according to Doris.

Although he had increased the support allowance several times in the course of the six years, Ralph was not complying fully with the escalator clause. Between his fear of Irene's finding out his actual current salary, which she was constantly threatening to do, and his guilt over withholding the full amount legally due her, he was in a constant stage of rage at her for, as he complained, "hanging on to me like a leech." One evening after a telephone fight with Irene that went on for an hour and a half, Doris asked, "I wonder who's hanging on to whom?" It was only then that he realized how involved he still was with his first wife, even after five years of a good remarriage, and how *he* as well as she was using the haggling over money to keep the relationship going. The next day he sent Irene a check for double the amount he had been sending her—the precise sum owed according to the escalator clause in the divorce agreement. Ralph reported that after he had done so he found himself exhilarated: "I felt a marvelous 'high,' as though a noose had been removed from my neck." Since then he has been able to handle those exasperating calls calmly, rationally—and briefly! Ralph, one can say, is finally divorced from Irene.

Part III

NEW LIVES

8
BACHELOR FATHER

A husband no longer, Father becomes a bachelor. He has to make a new life for himself, fill in the social gaps where friends who are more sympathetic to his ex-wife no longer see him. He must adjust to being single again. For one man this may be a frantic search for a good relationship with a woman. For another, "once burned, twice shy," it may be a slow, wary process. Often it means leaving the community of the married and joining the community of the divorced, or as Morton Hunt puts it, "the world of the formerly married." Here he discovers that he belongs to a distinct subdivision of this community—the divorced, single father—with its special problems.

Dating

The father who wants to keep his children close may be tempted to involve them too quickly in his new life. No matter what their age, children trying to absorb the trauma of divorce need the healing reassurance that Daddy still cares about *them.* Sure, they want to know about Daddy's life, but they want him for themselves; they don't want to compete for his affection and attention. Exposure to Father's relationships with women that are casual and impermanent may activate the ever-present fantasy that Mommy and Daddy will yet get together, since these women seem to come and go.

Once Father commits himself to a permanent relationship, he may want to introduce the new woman in his life to his children. He should be prepared for some strong reactions, depending upon the age, sex, and emotional development of each child and the relationship to the father.

Since the stability of the children's lives has already been disrupted once, any change may stir up old feelings, reawaken old fears. The intrusion into their lives of a person who is important to their father can threaten children of divorce. A cloud of doubt hovers over them. The echo of, Will he still care about us? is revived. The young child may react with the same rivalry that he would at the advent of a new brother or sister. Another child, torn by divided loyalties, may seek refuge in open hostility or feigned indifference to Father's new love. An adolescent boy may become openly competitive with his father.

Any and all of these reactions may also be influenced by the mother's attitude. She may be envious or resentful and undermine her children's trust in their father. Or she may use this new factor in the equation as an excuse to deny the father the right to see the children.

Many a father living with a woman may have reservations about openly acknowledging to his children the sexual relationship and may resort to a variety of devices intended to conceal it, such as having his girl friend stay away from the apartment while the children are visiting. Such subterfuges are usually not necessary. While children sometimes fight such a relationship, once they take it for granted, they can accept its ramifications. There is of course the risk that their mother may use this situation as a handy excuse to vent her unresolved hostility and refuse to allow her children to visit under these circumstances. In such instances discretion may be the better part of valor.

When Mother Objects

What is a father to do when his children's mother sets up roadblocks in his relationship with them? In Utopia all divorced mothers recognize the children's need for contact with their fathers. But in our world cooperation between divorced parents is not always forthcoming. Often the antagonism is so strong that the children's interests become secondary to the parents' need to continue their unresolved battles.

While most separation or divorce agreements contain the phrase "Parties will consult with each other about major issues relating to the children," if the parents are still enmeshed in their own hostility, such consultation can be of little value, leading only to further bitterness. Any issue can be the subject for disagreement. As we have seen, the mother may not permit her children to see their father on "moral grounds." The father may object to the type of school the mother has chosen; the mother may disapprove of the type of vacation the father has planned for the time his son is spending with him; but they may be unable to discuss this rationally ("He's not going to tell me what to do without paying for it" or "I spent seven years being pushed around by her and now I'm going to do what I want"). Until divorced parents resolve their hostilities, they will have to resort to their lawyers and the courts for help in settling those differences that loom as stalemates.

The child is the inevitable loser in these conflicts. He obviously needs someone to protect his interests, a spokesman whose concern would be what is best for the child. In their book *Parents Without Partners,* Jim and Janet Egleson recommended as long ago as 1961 that divorcing parents who foresee that there may be future difficulties they cannot resolve amicably should agree on a plan of arbitration. A professionally trained, objective person—someone well qualified in matters related to children—would be consulted in situations where parents differed, avoiding resort to legal action. Sadly, this good idea has not met with popular support.

Reactions to the Ex-Wife's Dating

Many a man is startled at his reaction to news of his ex-wife's dating. He finds himself curious about whom she is seeing and what she is doing. Even the man who is at last free of his emotional ties to his former wife may feel some stirrings of concern because of the children. Like our fictional Harry, he wonders: Who is that guy she's dating? Is that creep going to take my place in my children's home? Behind all the banter about finally being free of the alimony bag is the gnawing fear that someone will replace him and alienate his children. While as a divorced father you can't interfere with your ex-wife's choice of date or mate, your ongoing involvement with your children is your insurance against being displaced in their affections by anyone.

Adjusting to Two Lives—the Child's Dilemma

Often each divorced parent, either consciously or unconsciously, wants to be the preferred one, and in subtle ways conveys to the child the wish for top billing. This puts the child in a bind. It makes him feel that loyalty to one parent somehow means disloyalty to the other. He needs both parents. He also needs to feel that each parent recognizes his right to care about the other.

Your child has to adjust to two lives, his mother's and yours. A child may miss his mother while he is with you, especially on a happy occasion. This can be quite bewildering. In the midst of a gay Christmas party, five-year-old Jenny suddenly withdrew to a corner, clutching her presents and looking very sad. Her understanding Daddy put into words what she was feeling: "Are you unhappy you're not with Mommy? Would you like to tell her about your presents?" The tears that confirmed his suspicions were followed by the comforting reassurance that of course she could call Mommy. The father who is not threatened by evidence of his child's need for Mother and who conveys to the child his understanding of this feeling is contributing to acceptance by both father and child of their new design for living.

All children at some time or other try to use one parent against the other. Children whose lives have been disrupted by divorce are especially prone to this device. Surely, they reason, if Daddy doesn't like Mommy anymore, then he'll agree with me that Mommy is mean. Many a divorced father has been tempted to agree, thereby creating a closer alliance with his child. It is a hollow victory, for the child will undoubtedly feel guilty, the alliance will boomerang, and the child's sense of security with both parents will be diminished.

The first week after her parents separated, ten-year-old Wendy called her father and complained that Mommy said she couldn't watch TV because she hadn't finished her homework. Fortunately for Wendy, her father recognized this ploy of pitting one parent against the other and refused to become a party to it. For several weeks after, whenever Wendy visited her father, she tried to get Daddy to side with her in her differences with her mother. He listened to her complaints but always suggested she discuss the situation with her mother. When she realized that her father, though no longer married to her mother, supported her in her discipline, Wendy eventually gave up this manipulative maneuver.

If you cannot give your wholehearted support to your ex-wife's disciplinary measures, at least try to maintain an attitude of cautious skepticism when your children try to involve you in their complaints about their mother.

Many divorced fathers and mothers resent having their children tell them about their life with the other parent. They tend to see this as manipulative and hostile behavior (which in some instances it is). More often it may be the child's attempt to consolidate the two parts of his life. It may be hard to be a good listener at such a time, but Father can help the child sort out and reconcile the differences in tone, feeling, and style of the two households the child shares. Your child may fear that you will be disappointed to know he is happy when he is away from you. Let him know that you are pleased he is happy with his mother and that he doesn't have to compartmentalize his life.

Every child feels instinctively that he is part of each parent. He hears it in the remarks of friends and relatives: "She has her mother's eyes"; "He has his father's temper." If the parents disparage each other to the child, he cannot help but feel that, like the parent of whom he is a part, he must also be worthless. But how can you avoid discrediting your ex-wife to your children without being a hypocrite? After all, if she were all that wonderful, you wouldn't be divorced. Try to avoid discussing their mother's negative qualities with your young children, even when they bring the subject up. Without compromising your own feelings, you can help your children accept the reality that, while you and their mother each have faults and were not able to make a success of marriage, each of you can still be a good parent to them.

In the beginning you may find interweaving the strands of bachelorhood and fatherhood far from easy. But fathers tell us they have found that, as they began to settle down into their new life style, they and their children lost their edginess. With time, the new situation becomes familiar and more acceptable, and both father and children discover that their initial constrained reactions have eased and they are all feeling more comfortable together. You and the children are now a real family, just as your ex-wife and the children are a family—two families, where one existed before.

9 REMARRIAGE

Seventy-five percent of all divorces end in marriage. Having learned from past mistakes, the divorced person hopes that this time he will be able to make a better life. The father who is remarrying often worries that his remarriage may adversely affect his children. This casts a shadow on his own happiness. Yet remarriage doesn't *have* to mean emotional loss to the children. On the contrary, it can add a new dimension to their lives. Remarriage can create a whole home, give the children an opportunity to witness a happy marriage. Being exposed to a good relationship between two adults can alter a child's negative view of marriage and even exert a positive influence on his relationship with the opposite sex. His parents' remarriage can help put an end to any haunting feeling a child may have that his behavior was the cause of the divorce.

Divorce does deprive children of the opportunity for certain learning experiences. Remarriage can remedy this by exposing them to a loving, caring relationship, so that they will be able to get a positive concept of the husband-wife partnership and gain an understanding of the give-and-take, the compromises involved in any successful marriage.

Remarriage Opens New Possibilities

Remarriage creates a new family structure in which three or four people are now in the parent category. We have to view this new family structure in terms of gradation of parenthood, with the natural parents as The Parents. The role of the additional parent has been vague and confusing. The new man or woman in the household assumes the function of supplementary parent, who no more replaces the natural parent than does the child's teacher or counselor. New families give the child another chance to deal with the age-old problem of sharing the parents' love. In the course of time, as the child realizes that he hasn't lost this love, the new relationship can enrich his life.

New Relationships

What children call the additional parent is a matter of choice. Some children prefer using the first name; others use a nickname; still others combine the parental terms with the first name—Daddy Leo or Mommy Lynn. The form the children use is not important so long as it does not distort the reality that the stepparent is not the real parent. Being clear about whom they belong to will give children a better sense of their own identity.

Problems of Remarriage

The positive values of remarriage are experienced over a long period of time. The problems are felt immediately. A parent's remarriage, which creates another family, may reawaken all of a child's earlier insecurities and fears of loss. Even if you think your children have accepted the fact of remarriage, they need time to adjust to the actuality. While they are accepting a new man or woman in their lives, you can help them make their peace with this reality by reassuring them that your role in their lives will not be diminished by the introduction of a new person. Reassurance can only have meaning as a child experiences the parent's continuing involvement with him. No matter what age the children are, they should be made aware that the parent is marrying to satisfy his own needs for love and companionship that the children cannot be expected to supply.

Be prepared for a child's ambivalent feelings about the remarriage. Some children prefer having a parent just live with someone, for this arrangement seems less permanent than marriage and is less shattering to the child's fantasy that eventually his natural parents will be reunited. Often a child who has gotten along well with the parent's new partner will become hostile when the marriage becomes an actuality and may try to create friction between the couple. The parent has to realize that the child is not being a monster, but that he doesn't want a substitute parent and lacks the adult's motives to make the marriage work. The child may even feel that if he behaves disagreeably enough he may be able to break up the marriage, so that the longed-for reunion of his own parents will again be a possibility.

Reaction to the Ex-Wife's Remarriage

A former wife's remarriage can be a surprisingly turbulent experience for a divorced man. For the man who wanted out, the news brings with it a sense of release. He may be delighted to be free from the burden of alimony, but the delight and relief may also be tinged with resentment and envy, especially if he has not found a satisfactory companion. Since the general tendency is to feel that the divorce was the result of the other partner's failings, there also often comes a feeling of affront that after having botched up your life, your ex-partner has been able to find happiness.

Despite the obvious economic advantages, the change in his ex-wife's status may be a shock to a man's image of his parental role. Pained by the separation from his children and confronted by the reality of another man's living with them, he may resent having to support the children while another man enjoys the benefits of raising them. Sometimes a man feels so defeated that he even considers giving up his paternal rights, either by allowing his ex-wife's husband to adopt his children or, more commonly, by withdrawing from his children's lives. A father may reason, "They will be better off, there will be less confusion in their lives. It's easy enough to be a father when you're in the home. But being separated by time and space, and then displaced—who can fight that?"

If you are one of these men, tormented by the thought that someone else is going to tuck your children into bed at night, help them with their homework, decide how much TV they watch, what time they have to be home from dates; wondering, Where does that leave me? It's important that you re-examine your concept of fatherhood. Remember that what counts is your relationship with your child, a relationship that starts from the moment your child is born. Your ex-wife's remarriage, while it increases complexities, doesn't alter this basic reality.

Will They Like Him Better than Me?

Faced with a new man in your children's life, you may be concerned that they will turn toward him and away from you. In an effort to avert this, you may engage in a popularity contest, overindulging your children or, to put it more bluntly, trying to buy their loyalty and affection. You may hesitate to discipline them, fearful that they won't like you; and if they don't like you, you assume they will like the other man more. The most helpful thing a father can do for his children when his wife remarries is to be available to them, to continue to be a part of their lives.

This is a time when you can give your children a gift. You won't find it in a store and you can't order it by mail. It is your permission to like the new man in their lives. This is the most important present you can give them—a present that will help them accept and adjust to the changes in their family life. You can appreciate their reluctance to share their mother's love and interest with another person, but you can also emphasize the benefit to them of living in an intact home once again. They may grumble—he's too square, too old, too much or too little—but if you understand that they are using these minor targets to vent their anxiety that you will lose interest in them, you can place these criticisms in perspective and help your children cope with their changed situation.

Some children not only need their father's permission to like their mother's new husband, but they need to feel that their own father likes him as well. They may describe their stepfather in glowing terms, seeking your approval. You may feel differently. But you can help them understand that it is not necessary that you view him as they do, and that they are free to like whom they please.

Children's Reactions to Mother's Remarriage

There are children who encourage their mother to find another husband and long for her remarriage. Anticipating it as an answer to all their problems, they may, when it happens, become disillusioned all too soon. Frequently a child swings from one extreme to another before he achieves any sort of balance. You can help your children understand that it takes time for people, young and old, to find their way in new relationships.

In an effort to please his mother, a child may accept a stepfather too quickly, only to turn against him in short order when the child becomes troubled by his loyalty to his own father. The problem of divided loyalty is usually inspired by adults. Children carry their own radar. If you are worried that someone is taking your place in their lives, you may intensify their conflicts. If you can accept the fact that your children can have a relationship with many people, each of whom contributes to their well-being, you will be able to transmit this acceptance to your children and help them in their adjustment to their new family. The man who marries your children's mother is not their father, but neither is he only their mother's husband. As an additional parent he can supply a needed balance for your children, so that they are not burdened with an image of an all-powerful mother.

A child struggling to resolve the new relationships may find it too difficult to see his father during this period. You may be hurt and storm off ("If he doesn't want to see me, after all I've done for him, I'm through, and he can call me when he's good and ready"). Try to understand the child's predicament. Again, as the adult it is up to you to keep the lines of communication open. If your child doesn't want to see you, perhaps he will be more comfortable with a brief phone call or a note. Don't be afraid to take the initiative in showing your child your interest and in letting him know you understand that it takes time to work things out.

Coming to grips with their mother's remarriage, children often revert to an earlier ploy—using one parent against the other. Feeling threatened by the appearance of a new man, they may try to play one parent off against two, attempting to ingratiate themselves with their father by being critical of their mother or her husband, or both.

Keith was such a boy. Ten years old, he was very upset when his mother married Martin B. Martin was considerably older than Keith's father, with grown children. He didn't go to an office every day like Keith's father but stayed home and wrote. Big deal that his name was in magazines. He was always around; and when he was writing, Keith had to be quiet. Martin couldn't stand dogs. Topper was a barker. If someone even came near the driveway, he started to bark. Keith kind of liked it, because when just he and Topper were home alone, he felt very safe. But Martin would come storming out of his study: "Shut that dog up." All this got relayed to Daddy, who still had some vulnerable spots where Keith's mother was concerned. Immature, she had called him. She sure got herself a mature husband who couldn't even stand a dog. At first Eliot F., Keith's father, gave the boy a very sympathetic ear, but as the complaints continued and increased (Why did they have to move into Martin's big house in the country? He liked it better with Mommy in that little apartment in the city), Eliot realized that Keith was playing on his feelings and that he was falling for it. Sure, he'd been hurt. Nobody likes to be rejected. But if he wanted to be honest, he was a hell of a lot happier than when Dinah and he were married. He liked his free and easy life, and Dinah really seemed happy with Martin, which was certainly a change for Keith. When Keith's father was able to sort things out, he realized that Keith had been trying to enlist him as an ally in his attack on what he saw as an unnecessary intrusion in his life. As soon as Eliot stopped endorsing Keith's complaints and began to help the boy view his situation more realistically, Keith started to admit grudgingly that maybe living in the country was better for Topper (he had more room to run) and that it was true he had more fun now that Mom was happier.

The Child's Reactions According to His Developmental Stage

The toddler, in his effort to free himself from dependence on his mother, may turn to the available male figure in the house.

His lap may be the one sought to satisfy the child's need for closeness with someone other than the mother. This doesn't mean the child is turning away from his natural father. It means he is seeking the comfort and strength he needs where it is available.

But divorce brings with it heightened sensitivity, particularly for the divorced father of the young child, who has only had a brief time to be with his child before being separated. Such a father often finds it difficult to accept another man's being close to his child. It is well to remember that, throughout a child's development, there may be periods when he leans more toward the man in the home and other periods when he will turn toward his own father. The father who doesn't feel threatened by this will be able to appreciate that his child is gaining from the opportunity to develop warmth for and confidence in more than one male.

Both boys and girls may see the new man in the family as a rival for Mother's affection and attention. If an ex-wife remarries during your children's early years (two to five), when a son is struggling with his wishes to possess his mother, the boy may react with anger when he realizes he must share her. Until the intruder came on the scene, the divorce may have encouraged the boy's feelings that he had succeeded in keeping Mother to himself. Often, in the early stages of divorce, a mother, in her loneliness, may encourage the idea in her child that he is all she has, the only thing that gives meaning to her life. Her interest in a new man may make the child feel there is something wrong with *him*. If he were good enough, Mother wouldn't need anyone else. She really must not love him. Often, when a child feels insecure with one parent, he will turn to the other for comfort. Your son who feels unlovable and rejected, your daughter who feels envious of her mother's attention to her new husband, will need your reassurance to help them over this hurdle.

Then there is the adolescent boy who is struggling with his need to establish his independence and emancipation from his family. His mother's remarriage can reawaken his earlier conflicts. It is at this time that an adolescent boy may express a desire to live with his father. This wish has to be evaluated carefully. Is the young man trying to punish his mother for her unfaithfulness to him, or is he seeking to be spared exposure to a situation he may find too stimulating and disturbing? It may indeed be in his best interests to be with his father at this time.

Parents' Attempts to Handle Social Situations

When the mother remarries and the bitterness of the divorce has abated, some parents, united by their concern for their children, try to maintain a friendly relationship. Phyllis's mother, who was remarried, explained that it seemed only natural to invite her ex-husband in for a drink when he brought six-year-old Phyllis home after her visit with him. The mother did not realize how confusing it was for Phyllis, until one day the child asked why, since they all had such a good time together, Daddy couldn't come and live with them. He could sleep in the extra bed in her room. She wouldn't mind that she couldn't have friends for sleep-overs!

Older children can handle this situation better. We have known adolescents who felt more comfortable when their parents behaved in a casually friendly way. Before any joint social meetings are planned, however, they should be thoroughly discussed with the children.

When Father Remarries

Father's remarriage places him in yet another role. Once again a husband, but still a father to his children, he faces new complications (these are discussed in Chapter 10). The irony of the new situation is that what is bringing him such happiness is creating anxiety for his children, which casts a cloud over his own pleasure.

It is a rare child who accepts Father's remarriage with equanimity. Many fathers need their children's approval of their remarriage, and they may press for immediate acceptance. Like your children, you may be torn. You want to be with your new wife. You want to be with your children. You have dreams about what a happy time you will all have together. What a good influence your new wife will be on your children. She has so much to contribute. You can't wait for them to get what she has to offer. But your children are uncooperative. They are negative and cool. Your dreams explode.

Depending on their temperament, children exhibit their reactions to remarriage in different ways. Some express their feelings directly, others more subtly. But be prepared—whatever their feelings, they will be strong. Old fears of desertion that your child experienced when he was told you and his mother planned to separate may be reawakened. This reaction may come as a shock to you. Hadn't you shown him by your actions that his fears were unfounded? How much proof does he need? And hadn't he been the one who'd been asking when you and Julie were going to get married? Of course, you never were completely sure how he really felt about her. They seemed to hit it off. Yet sometimes on a weekend, when you told him Julie was joining you for dinner, there would be the question "Does she have to?" Taking your cue from that, you would decide to devote the next weekend to your son, only to have him ask, "Isn't Julie coming with us? Why don't we call her?" Who can figure out a kid like that? You'll have to try. It is confusing because your child is torn by conflicting feelings. He wants you. He wants you to want him, but at the same time he may be afraid that, if he comes between you and your new love, you will be angry with him. He may be convinced when he is with you that you do care about him, but when faced with competition, his conviction falters. He fears now you will become absorbed in your own life and forget that you have a son.

A five-year-old boy, told of his father's plans to marry, asked, "Will you still be my father? Will I still see you?" While these questions may be painful for you to hear, the more you can encourage your child to express his doubts and fears, the more he will eventually be able to cope with the situation.

A father's remarriage rings the death knell on the child's persistent fantasy that his parents will get together again. Now the child has to make peace with the new reality. But before he does, he may express his frustration and fear of loss and rejection in a variety of ways. For instance, you may be startled and a little impatient when your very independent seven-year-old daughter begins to act like a four-year-old during visits after your remarriage. Suddenly she becomes very clinging; she may call you into her room repeatedly after she has gone to bed; insist on getting into your bed in the morning; interrupt any conversation you may be having with your wife. Despite your annoyance, you may understand your daughter's anxiety and put up with it, but your wife may have less patience with your interfering visitor.

Your children may try to avoid seeing you or may behave rudely to your new wife. They may try to provoke you, to test your acceptance. Their very behavior may push you to the outer limits, where you may well wonder, What is the point of putting up with this? At last I've found some happiness for myself, and these kids are going to mess it up for me.

Stepchildren and stepparents are strangers to one another. Acceptance is a slow process that does not respond to pressure. Try to see your children's behavior as a transitory phase; peaceful coexistence takes time.

Feelings Stirred Up in Mother

Your children have to cope with their mother's feelings about your remarriage as well as their own. This event can be the spark to ignite her unresolved hostilities or her dependence on you, which she may project onto her concern about the financial arrangements ("How can you support two families?"). Complaints about the inadequacy of child support and alimony may be revived. She is justifiably worried: you may very well have to provide less. She sees your new wife taking something away from her and the children (even though the new wife may have to work in order to allow you to support your children). She is afraid you will gradually forgo your interest in and responsibility for your children. If the mother is particularly resentful, she may bring about the very thing she fears. Her misgivings may increase the children's anxiety about the loss of their father, intensifying their hostility toward him with the eventual outcome that the father grows more and more remote.

If your ex-wife is so resentful of your new life, feeling that any expenditure you make on your new wife is depriving your children, it is up to you to explain to your children that you are doing your best to care for them. Explanations are important, but more important is your understanding of the conflict the children are caught in. Most important is the unspoken message they receive from you. If you continue to participate in their lives, are aware of their need to have time alone with you, and allow them to make a relationship with your new wife at their own pace, your children will find the reassurance they need to quiet their anxieties.

Along the Road to Adjustment—the Role of Father's Wife

The Cinderella story has a universal appeal because it touches something familiar to all children. Mothers are good *or* bad in the eyes of their young children. When the good mother has to deny or frustrate the child's wishes, she becomes for that moment the bad mother. The wicked stepmother is such a popular figure with children because she embodies all the qualities of the bad mother, enabling them to see their mother as the good one. Hating the stepmother frees children from the guilt and confusion they experience when they are angry with the mother they also love and need. With the introduction of Father's new wife into his life, a young child has a ready-made target for negative feelings—the wicked stepmother who can do only wrong. The stepmother may have a hard time until the child is able to see her as the person she really is. She must be prepared for the slow process of adjustment that will, it is hoped, lead to a comfortable relationship for her, her husband, his children, and their mother.

The child who is still very close to his mother needs to be approached very tentatively by the stepmother. She is not just any adult to him; she is someone coming between him and his father, someone who may take Father away from him. She must be prepared to offer love and warmth for a long time without receiving anything in return except at most an ungracious tolerance.

The child is not the only one who has mixed feelings. Stepmothers have their share. Carolyn F. describes how it is from her position as stepmother:

"Stu's kids are lots of fun. I really like to have them come. But it's never out of my mind that they are hers. Not that they let me forget it. They're always talking about Mommy, constantly reminding me that Stu had a life before me. I know she resents me and talks against me. You can tell from the kids' behavior when they first come in. It takes them a while to unwind—and I do mean unwind: it's as if they have to disentangle themselves from their ties to her and what she feels. So I try to be really nice to prove she's wrong about me. I always try to have the kind of food they like, and sometimes I'll slip in an extra snack that I know they aren't allowed to have at home. Like sodas. I figure maybe I'll chalk up some extra Brownie points with them."

Those Brownie points may well be a boomerang. Children understand all too well the art of playing one parent against the other, getting what they want, learning how to be manipulative. But it weakens their relationship with the adult, whom they see as someone to be conned.

The new wife can't be faulted for trying. She knows how important the children are to her husband and that if they have a good relationship with her, it will add to her husband's pleasure. Sometimes she tries too hard, like Carolyn. She might then ask herself: "Am I trying to replace the mother because of my feelings of rivalry? Am I guilty about my resentment of the time and money my husband spends on his children? Am I afraid he is more interested in his children than he is in me?" The stepmother's role is a difficult one; but if she is honest with herself, she will be more able to be patient until the children develop positive feelings for her.

Stepmother to the Adolescent

If you remarry when your children are approaching or are already in adolescence, they will probably react with the ambivalence that marks this stage of their development. They may be fascinated by your new life. Whether or not your new wife is younger than their mother, she is probably different from her, and they may find an excitement in your life that contrasts sharply with what they have been experiencing at home. Their inconsistent behavior may puzzle you. One moment they seem to enjoy being with you, the next they are surly and unpleasant. These abrupt mood swings may reflect the pull of divided loyalties. Your children may feel disloyal to their mother when they are having a good time with you and your wife. Your ex-wife, threatened by the possibility that your new wife will displace her in the children's affections, may compound their guilt by her reaction. She may be critical of one whom she views as a competitor and thus arouse in the children the fear that "if we like her, Mother will be angry, and if we don't, Father will be displeased with us." If the children are fortunate enough to have parents who understand their need to be a part of the lives of both parents, they will be able to cope with this conflict. Make it clear to your children that, while you hope they will find a place in their lives for one whom you care for, you do not expect her to displace their mother.

The Adolescent Girl and Her Stepmother

Your adolescent daughter will undoubtedly include your wife in the maelstrom of her reactions. In the conflict between her push to independence and the pull of dependency—in her wish to let go and the fear of letting go—your daughter is trying to wean herself from her mother. Competing with her, attempting to prove she is a better woman, is one of the ways the adolescent girl strives to achieve this independence. She may displace this competition onto your wife, thus allowing herself to deny any hostile feelings toward her mother.

She may see your new wife as a successful rival for your affection. Her buried childhood desires for her father may be reawakened, stimulated perhaps by the atmosphere of loving sexuality in your new marriage. In her struggle to cope with these wishes and to accept their frustration, your daughter may behave in a way that leaves you very perplexed. For example, a thirteen-year-old girl came to the luxurious apartment of her father, a designer, and his new wife, a model, looking like a waif, unkempt, dirty, sandals tied with string. Shy, uncommunicative, she had no other way to express her anger at her father for leaving her for "another woman."

On the other hand, she may admire your wife excessively, bringing back tales of her talents and superiority to torment her mother. You and your wife may be pleased by this admiration; your children's mother, on the other hand, may find the praise with its implicit criticism of her difficult to bear. But if all the adults involved do not take this behavior at face value, they will realize that the adolescent daughter's criticism of her mother is her stock in trade. If there were no new wife, if her parents were living together, you may be sure the adolescent girl would find other ways to put her mother down.

Your daughter may subject your wife to the same alternation of feeling she exhibits toward her mother. Your wife may well have little tolerance for this; she may be tempted to withdraw from the relationship and, perhaps unconsciously, to encourage your withdrawal. This will undoubtedly be a difficult period for you; but if you can hang in there until your daughter has overcome her initial resentment toward your wife, she may find a companionship that will give her pleasure. It can also defuse the intensity of her relationship with her mother. A remarried father, talking about the adjustment of his fifteen-year-old daughter to his remarriage, put it very well: "In some ways, Emily has the best of both worlds. When she feels her mother is getting into her hair, she comes to our house and raps with Lois (my wife), who's the big women's libber Emily'd like her mother to be."

The Adolescent Boy and Stepmother

The adolescent boy also goes through a period of rivalry with the parent of the same sex. Your remarriage can intensify this rivalry. A young and pretty stepmother can arouse his sexual feelings and fantasies. He may be charming and ingratiating, yet later become so upset by his guilt over his seductive feelings or fantasies that he may insist on seeing his father only when the new wife isn't present or, in more extreme situations, try to avoid seeing his father at all. A young man can find strength to cope with his confused and guilty feelings if the stepmother doesn't respond to seductive overtures and if his father makes very clear that she is *his* woman. A stepmother who does not try to compete with the natural mother or interfere in her husband's relationship with his son will find that there are many gratifying possibilities open to her as friend and confidante to her husband's son and his friends.

Two Homes or One?

Many divorced fathers find it hard to face the fact that their children's lives are different as a result of remarriage. They would like to deny that their children now live in two worlds; to believe nothing has changed. When a father remarries, it is hard for him to accept the reality that his new home is not his children's home.

Children need a base that is home. Some fathers want their children who live with their mother to feel that Dad's house is also the children's home, i.e., that they have two homes. This insistence that the children should believe they have two homes only emphasizes that they live in a divided world. Your home can be a place where they feel comfortable, accepted, loved–in short, where they feel *at home.* But their home is at their mother's.

10
THE EXTENDED FAMILY

Mine, yours, ours—ordinary possessive pronouns. But when applied to the familial relationships of divorced parents, what a complexity of problems and pleasures they embrace. The extended family encompasses a variety of combinations. The situation can be simple—a father whose children live with his ex-wife remarries and has children by his second wife; or moderately complex—a father whose children live with their mother marries a woman with children by a former marriage who live with her; or multiplex—both parents marry partners with children from previous marriages and go on to have children of their own. Any of these marriages brings, in all probability, collateral relatives—parents, sisters, brothers, uncles, aunts, and cousins of the new spouse.

Extended Families Open New Possibilities

Students of the family are constantly bemoaning the isolation and burden under which the nuclear family functions. Many people refer nostalgically to the benefits of the large, extended family of past eras. Remarriage provides the possibility of additional family relationships that can ease the tensions inherent in the small, self-contained family unit.

Accustomed to the nuclear family, you may wonder how your children can absorb all the new relationships. The integration of the extended family can only be achieved with effort and patience. But the rewards are worth the hard work. Anxiety, conflict, and frustration are a part of growth that all children have to experience. The extended family gives them an additional opportunity to resolve conflicts and accept frustration while at the same time providing the possibility for a wider variety of satisfying relationships.

It is difficult for a child to surrender his position in the family. Every parent of more than one child can corroborate this with stories of the first child's undisguised resentment at being displaced by a new sibling. Children whose parents' remarriage involves them in an extended family often resent having to forfeit their role as oldest, youngest, or only child. But an only child who lacks the companionship of sisters and brothers may, after having resolved his feelings of rivalry and displacement, enjoy the involvement with stepsisters and stepbrothers. A young child may profit from acquiring an older stepbrother or stepsister who can serve as a model. It is not uncommon, when there is rivalry and tension between the two sets of children, that the birth of a half sister or half brother serves as the rallying point for the family.

One father recounted the fights between his daughter and his wife's daughter. However, the girls' common meeting ground was the new baby boy, who now had "three loving mothers." Also, in extended family units children often find an additional aunt, uncle, or grandparent who may bring more love and caring into their lives or add some special or unusual facet of interest.

Not just children but also adults gain from the potentialities of extended relationships. Your wife's children cannot have the same meaning for you as your own do; and if you do not expect your feelings to be the same, you will be able to derive satisfaction from the new role you have come heir to—whether mentor, confidant, or friend. Rarely are the pleasures and advantages of the extended family experienced immediately. The father who expects instant adjustment is doomed to disappointment.

Problems Your Children Face

If you marry a woman whose children live with you, don't be surprised if your children feel jealous of them. Fearful that you will prefer your new wife's children to them, they may become competitive, and try to show you how much better or smarter they are. Or, angry at the competitors who have usurped their Daddy, they may test your love by refusing to see you altogether.

When your children come to visit, you may be eager for all the children to be together in one big happy family. But until your children feel their place in your life is safe, they will not welcome any intrusion into their time with you. Plan your time in such a way that at least part of it is spent alone with them.

A mother of two sons told how her older boy, age thirteen, sensitively withdrew when her husband's boys visited, allowing the father to be alone with his own children. However, her younger son, age eight, who enjoyed being with his stepfather, resented not being included in the father's outings with his own children.

Shared experiences with both sets of children, whether they be a picnic, preparing a meal together, painting a fence, washing the family car, or cleaning out the garage, can be important in creating the fabric of family feeling. But wait until your children feel at home with your new family before introducing these activities.

The New Baby

If you and your wife have a baby, the introduction of a half sibling may heighten your children's insecurity and temporarily underline their fear of being displaced. In some situations, such as the one described earlier, the new baby can become a cohesive force for the family. Your children may see the new baby as a sign of the permanence of your relationship and in accepting this their security is increased. Seeing you play with your new child as you have played with them, they may re-experience the pleasures of your fathering them. Watching Father trot around with baby Tad on his shoulder, Barry remarked with a grin, "I remember when I was little and you put me on your shoulders."

Strangers to You—Relatives to Your Child

There are people who play a role in your children's lives, yet may be strangers to you. These are the relatives they acquire when their mother remarries. Don't try to turn your children off when they want to talk about their stepsisters, half brothers, or other new relations. If you are receptive, it will not only help your children work out their feelings about these new people in their lives but will also encourage them to realize there are no forbidden areas in their relationship with you, that they can be comfortable about mixing their two worlds.

Different Life Styles

Your children may have to adjust to two very different life styles. Your home may be more organized, more formal than their mother's. In your household the children may be expected to participate in chores, while at their mother's these demands are not made on them. Children are flexible and can adjust to this if there is consistency within the home—if they know that at Daddy's house we always make our beds and that in our house we do as we please. The adaptability of the child is known to any parent whose children have ever had friends visit for a few days. Within short order the young guest identifies himself with your home, referring to your house as "our house."

Children may like one life style better than another, but they can accept this fact. Just as they may come home from a visit with a friend complaining, "They're very strict, only one hour of TV," it is rare that the complaints interfere with their accepting another invitation to visit if they really like the friend. If your children are able to resolve their competitive feelings, secure in their meaning for you, they will be able to cope with differences in life styles. Prolonged complaints and difficulties about these differences may indicate deeper unresolved conflicts to which parents should be attentive.

You as Stepfather

As the new man in the house, you have to chart your own course. If you have married a woman with children hoping they wouldn't intrude upon your life, you are in for a rude awakening. As long as you share a home with your wife, you will have to face sharing your wife with her children. You may feel deprived because of your wife's interest in and concern for her children and think you don't count at all. Or you may be tempted to assume the role of substitute parent. If their father is a vague shadow in the children's life, this temptation is very strong; you may indeed be filling a need by acting as a surrogate father. But if the father is around to assert his place in his children's lives, you will have to make your own special relationship.

Your best counsel can only come from an awareness of your own motives. Being the parent in residence offers many temptations to supplant, rather than supplement, the natural father. Living with your wife's children may intensify the pain you experience at being separated from your own children. You feel deprived and turn to your stepchildren for compensation. You may compete with your stepchildren's father, trying to deny your stepfatherhood by assuming the role of an over-indulgent father. One stepfather we know, who saw his own child very infrequently because she lived in another part of the country, could not understand why he felt uncomfortable if he happened to answer the phone when his stepdaughter's father called. As he discussed his situation he began to realize that, pleased with the warm parental relationship he had with his stepdaughter, he had been unconsciously encouraging her hostility to her father, rationalizing that he *was* a difficult man. It was not hard for him to understand that it was his guilt about his desire to displace the natural father that made him so uncomfortable at any contact with him.

Perhaps your own children are giving you a hard time because of your remarriage, and, without being aware of it, you may be expressing your resentment toward them by being overstrict or impatient with your stepchildren. Or you may want the children for your own; want them to feel you are their father, if only to prove to your wife how much you care about her and hers.

The stepfather who tries so hard to replace the real father in the child's affection may become resentful when, despite all his efforts, the child continues to long for his real father. As one stepfather said in desperation, "No matter how much I do for him, he's impossible to live with when he doesn't hear from his father, who's just an irresponsible bum." It may be hard for you to recognize that for your own reasons you don't want to face the child's need for his natural father. You will stand a better chance of achieving a more meaningful relationship with your stepchildren if they know you feel they have a right to love their real father more. Neither you nor the children will be hampered by guilt, and together you will be able to work out a role for yourself that will meet their needs and yours.

The essential question is whether the child is confused by having two fathers and whether his loyalties are strained. Often adults are more confused than the children. Diane, a ten-year-old girl we know, showed her teacher the new sweater she got from her father for her birthday. After admiring the sweater, the teacher, knowing she had a stepfather, asked, "Which father gave it to you?" Diane's response might be a guide for the confused adult. "I only have one *father*," she said, adding as an afterthought, "some people have lots of stepfathers."

Your Stepchildren's Reactions to You

As a stepfather you will be trying to find your way in a situation that has a haunting familiarity. The envy, the competition, the fear of loss, the anger at having to share a parent are all there. You feel as if you are looking into mirrors. Only this time it is not your children who are testing and mistrustful. These are strangers with whom you don't share a background of experience or close feelings but with whom you share a home and the intimacy of day-to-day living.

Your wife's son may repeatedly test your interest in him by annoying behavior. But if you are able to keep your cool, neither overreacting to his provocations nor trying to win his favor by being overpermissive, the little boy will begin to accept you and the benefits of having a man in the house once again.

Your wife's daughter, like all girls, may try to compete with her mother to prove she can be a better wife. As a well-meaning stepfather you may fall right in with this and even do a little wooing on your own in the mistaken belief that in this way you will be able to win favor with your stepdaughter. Unfortunately, this can only add to her confusion by building up her hopes—as well as her fears—that she is the desired one. The cautious stepfather knows he has to go slowly in forming a relationship with his wife's children. He understands that he is regarded as an intruder who has to prove himself. He must be prepared to accept the spoken or unspoken "Who needs you?" The stepfather can do more than merely accept outbursts. He can help the children by not promising too much. "Give me a chance to love you and be a father to you" can be very upsetting to a child who feels one father is enough to cope with. A more realistic "Let's give it a chance and get to know each other" can be less threatening and more reassuring to a child.

Grandparents

Grandparents can play an important part in the life of the child of divorced parents. Children feel their roots shaken by divorce. Their world is changed. They are suddenly catapulted into membership in a club they did not choose—Children of Divorced Parents. Ties to relatives are particularly important at this time. By giving a sense of continuity to a child's life, grandparents can be a steadying influence. They are there for the child to turn to as they were before the divorce. Mother and Father may be preoccupied in making new lives for themselves, too caught up in their own emotional turmoil to give their children the support they need. Grandparents can fill this gap by providing a receptive ear, an oasis of comfort, the neutral support that can be balm to the wounds inflicted by the children's divided loyalties.

Many grandparents find it hard to achieve neutrality, involved as they are in their own hostility to the son- or daughter-in-law who may have rejected their own child. Sometimes their hostility is a carry-over from the predivorce situation. Often they feel angry or disappointed in their own child, and in order to maintain a workable relationship with their son or daughter, they project their angry feelings onto the former in-law. Difficult as it may be, if the grandparents can detach themselves from the emotional bitterness that is the residue of any divorce, they can help to give their grandchildren a perspective that can strengthen their ability to avoid being involved in an emotional tug-of-war.

Eight-year-old Alec was fortunate in having a paternal grandmother who recognized how important it was for him that she remain outside the fray. Alec resented going on vacation with his mother, his stepfather, and his two stepbrothers (they lived with their mother), whom he didn't like. He reported to his grandmother that he had told his mother he didn't want to go, but she said it wasn't up to him to make the decision. Grandmother let him talk about how he disliked the arrangement, but she did not let her sympathy for Alec interfere with what she knew was her proper role—to be neutrally supportive without disagreeing with Alec's mother. She helped Alec accept the fact that it wasn't his decision at this point. When he got older he would be able to make his own decisions, but in the meantime Grandmother discussed with him ways in which he could avoid letting the other children spoil his fun.

If grandparents are hostile toward their ex-daughter-in-law, if they are critical of her life style, it will create a barrier that grandchildren may find difficult to overcome. Sensing the hostility, the children will avoid discussing what may be a significant part of their lives, and the grandparents will be giving up their important role as good listeners. It has been our experience that those grandparents who manage a good relationship with their former daughters-in-law do so by putting first things first. As one grandmother said, "She is my grandchildren's mother, and we know that if we want to continue to be close to our grandchildren—and they are very important to us—we have to make every effort to maintain a friendly relationship with her."

Sometimes grandparents complain that their grandchildren, who before the divorce were very loving and devoted, now resent their presence. What often emerges is that the grandparents are unaware that they are intruding on their grandchildren's relationship with their father. Particularly if the children are young and the divorce is new, the children may be reluctant to share their father with the grandparents. In such situations perhaps the grandparents can arrange to see the grandchildren at a different time, so they can avoid competing with their son for the children's interest.

Steprelatives

Through your remarriage you have undoubtedly acquired additional family. Until your children have accepted their stepmother, it is not likely they will immediately be receptive to her parents or other relatives. As we have stressed, adults and children have to feel their way. It will take time and patience for a comfortable relationship to flourish.

If you have married a woman with children, your parents may not be ready to accept these instant grandchildren. There will undoubtedly be a difference between the way they feel toward these children and the way they feel toward your children. Everyone involved should recognize and respect this difference. As grandparents and children get to know one another better, the relationship will reflect the feeling that has developed.

Part IV

FATHERS AND SONS AND DAUGHTERS

11
FULL-TIME FATHER

What about the separated or divorced father whose children live with him? Although most children of divorce live with their mothers, a significant number live with their fathers. Who are these fathers and children? How do they manage together?

Until recently, a child of "tender years" was almost always placed in the custody of the mother unless there was clear evidence of her being physically, mentally, or morally unfit to look after the child. A mother, it was reasoned, besides providing "mother love," that precious nutrient for the young child's healthy growth, was better able to care for the child than the father since she stayed home and would be readily available to her child.

A closer look at these assumptions has raised some question as to their validity. Leaving aside for the moment the age-old belief that biological motherhood and maternal love go hand in hand, the facts are that, of the female work force in the United States, almost half are mothers of children under eighteen; six million of these working mothers have children under six. With increasing numbers of mothers working outside the home and with more and more fathers asserting their wish—and their right—to raise their children, other things being equal, many judges are beginning to give more weight in custody fights to the father's claim to custody, even of the young child.

Father as Custodial Parent

Custody of 10 to 15 percent of children under eighteen is awarded by the court to the father at the time of the divorce proceedings. Custody is never final. A noncustodial parent can reopen the matter of custody any time there is a radical change in the circumstances of the custodial parent (such as moving a long distance away, remarriage, mental illness) or, for that matter, a change in his own circumstances. (For example, sometimes upon remarriage a father will ask for custody of a child because he thinks the child will be better off with him now.) If the father as noncustodial parent can prove it is indeed in the child's best interests that custody be transferred to him, the court may so decree. Statistics on the number of children whose legal custody is transferred to the father after the divorce are unavailable, but from what judges tell us the number is considerable.

In addition to those children awarded to the father by the court in the course of a custody battle, the custody of some children is given to the father without a struggle by the mother. There is, for example, the occasional woman, desperate to get out of an intolerable marriage, who will relinquish the children in exchange for her freedom. And there is a small but growing number of women who willingly hand over the children to the father to free themselves from the responsibility of child care or for some other personal reason, such as to go off with a lover.

Many judges allow adolescents, considered young adults, to choose the parent they want to live with, and a not inconsiderable number opt for Father. Then again, some parents agree to split custody of the children, with one child or more going to live with the father.

Besides these children, there are many who come to live with Father at a later time, although the mother remains the nominal custodial parent. Among these are children whose mothers, through necessity or choice, send them to the father —with or without his consent. One mother, exasperated at her ex-husband for defaulting on his support payments, sent their two children, ages ten and twelve, halfway across the country to their father and his second family, informing him only when the children were already aboard the plane. Some separated or divorced mothers who manage to handle the troubles of their children while they are small find themselves so overwhelmed by their problems when the children get older that in desperation they send the offspring to their father as the only viable solution. One mother, whose fifteen-year-old son didn't get along with his new stepfather, asked his father to take him because he threatened the stability of her remarriage.

Sometimes a mother will hand over a sick or handicapped child to the father if he is in a better position than she to take care of him. In our experience we have found that the custody of deviant children, though awarded by the court to the mother, is not infrequently assumed by the father at a later time either when the situation of one or the other parent changes, as, for example, when the mother remarries and the stepfather objects to the child, or when the mother finds the burden too heavy to carry alone.

Then there are always those youngsters in the custody of their mothers who, upon arriving at adolescence, with all its *sturm und drang,* think that pastures are greener at Father's and in one way or another manage to transfer their place of residence to his. Many a father has been surprised to find his adolescent son or daughter sometimes literally sitting on his doorstep, having run away from home to stay with him.

Let us take a closer look at these situations in which the father is awarded legal custody.

When Mother Deserts

When a woman finds her marriage unendurable, for whatever the reasons, society expects her to take the children with her if she leaves the home. It is with a sense of incredulity that we hear of a mother who has run off and left the children. Fathers who desert their families are no rarity. (Welfare rolls are replete with women and children abandoned by the breadwinner.) We greet news of a father's defection with head-shaking clucks of disapproval or expressions of indignation or, among some groups, with just plain resignation—"That's how men are." But there is something morally repugnant to most of us about a mother who abandons her children, especially, as most frequently happens, to go off with another man.

Although we are familiar with reports of mothers who run away and never see their children again, all of those with whom we had experience did get in touch with their children either by phone, letter, or in person within a few weeks. They longed for them and returned, if not to the household they had abandoned, at least to see the children to assure them of their love and to try to re-establish themselves in their hearts. Several fought for custody in the subsequent divorce proceedings and succeeded in obtaining it or at least in getting joint custody (often a euphemistic term to save face for the mother who has visiting privileges but whose children remain in the physical custody of the father). However, if the father contests such a mother's request for custody of the children—whether from revenge or because he believes it is in their best interests—he can generally obtain it by having the mother declared "morally unfit" as evidenced by her desertion of the children (even though, up to the moment of leaving, she had been a nurturing, loving mother, quite as "fit" to care for the children after the act, shocking though it was, as before).

It is a bitter blow to a man's self-esteem to have his wife leave him and the children. The pain, the humiliation, can only be borne with the help of such comforting thoughts as "she's just a whore," "good riddance to bad rubbish," or, in the fashionable psychiatric parlance of today, "she must be sick."

Children have no such solace. All they know is that their mother, whom they love, and on whom they depend, has abandoned and betrayed them. Bereft of their mother, they are acutely vulnerable at this time to the terror of being abandoned by their father as well. For they feel somehow responsible for Mother's departure. How many times, exasperated by their disobedience, had she threatened to go away and leave them? They had paid no attention, kept on being "bad." Now they were punished.

Seeing a father sad, little children mistake his sadness or withdrawal as anger or rejection of them. Surely, they think, you must be angry with them for making Mother go away. You can punish them by leaving too. You naturally assume that the children know they can count on you—that they take for granted your concern, your reliability. They may not take it for granted at all, especially if they are very young. At such a terrible time children need concrete evidence of your love and dependability, frequent and convincing assurance that you will take care of them and never leave. You will want to be with them as much as possible and continue your activities together much as before. Your mutual love and support should bring some calm to this turbulent time.

There is, of course, the immediate task of finding an adequate person to look after the children and of righting the household turned topsy-turvy by the absence of the homemaker. Coping with the household minutiae—getting the kids dressed, fed, and off to school, shopping for groceries, taking care of the laundry; the dishes stacked in the sink, the cut on Amy's finger, Susie's tangled hair, the rip in Bobby's pants—all on top of a full day's work is a pretty grim load for a stunned man. In some ways, though, having to tend to these physical details can help dull, at least while you're busy with them, the anger and pain and leave you less time for self-pity or breast beating.

Difficult, harassing, burdensome—and costly!—as the practical problems are, they are minor compared to your job of helping the children absorb the blow of their mother's defection and still keep their faith in her love for them. Children feel not only unloved when a parent leaves but also unlovable. This is particularly true when the departing parent is the mother.

Try not to run the mother down. This is a big order. In your hurt it is very tempting to stress her faults, seek comfort in turning the children against her. For it is not easy, under the emotional burden of your own distress, to speak any way but disparagingly of her in the face of the reality of her abandonment. But this approach can only add to the children's hurt, and it ignores their need to continue to believe in her love for them and in her return.

In your bitterness it is an even harder sacrifice to allow her to see or even speak to the children when she returns. "She left them," you may justify your denial of her request. "She has no right to see them." This reaction overlooks the children's need to hear from her, to feel she still cares for them.

Not infrequently a child will refuse to see or talk with the mother either out of loyalty to the father or as punishment of her for her abandonment. This in no way means the child has banished the mother from his heart or his mind. Indeed, thoughts of a departed parent, whether lost by death, divorce, or desertion, will often preoccupy a child, color his daydreams, and even influence his behavior. Paradoxically, children often unconsciously take into themselves the character, the manner, even the interests of the absent parent, as if by so doing they can keep the parent close to them. Your consent to the children's seeing their mother, whether or not they do so, will be a comfort and a help to them in the long run.

Your own relationship to the children is bound to be affected by your changed role as father-mother. One father said that at the beginning he found himself oversolicitous of the children and preoccupied with fears that some other disaster might befall them. Another said he was overstrict and compulsively checked up on them from his office or whenever he was away from home for any length of time. Eventually such fathers settle into the role of double parent with some degree of success.

When Mother Is "Mentally Unfit"

When the mother is psychotic or so mentally disturbed that she cannot, or indeed should not, be the custodian of the children, the court generally awards custody to the father. If the mother becomes severely ill mentally while she is the custodial parent, the father can request a change of custody.

In addition to the practical problems of arranging for the children's care if you are in a position to have them stay with you while Mother is ill, you are faced with the task of helping your children comprehend what has happened to their mother and to understand whatever bizarre or irrational or ambiguous behavior they may have been subjected to while living with her during her illness. Children who have been living with or exposed to a mentally disturbed parent are likely to be more vulnerable to the vicissitudes of a one-parent home than other children. They will need more of your time to counterbalance the shaky, uncertain, or confusing situation to which they have been subjected and to give them a feeling of trust and stability in the adults around them.

The children should be encouraged to keep in touch with their mother, if only by a brief letter or postcard, with the expectation that she will recover and re-establish a going relationship with them, whether or not they ever return to live with her again. Keep alive the memory of whatever good times they had with her when she was well and the hope that she will be in good health again.

When Mother Willingly Relinquishes Custody

Until not so many years ago a mother who *voluntarily* relinquished custody of the children to the father was a rare bird indeed. Today, matrimonial lawyers tell us, such women are cropping up in their practice in increasing numbers. Under the impetus of the women's liberation movement, women—and men, too—are beginning to question their time-honored roles in society as daughter, sister, wife, mother; to re-evaluate basic assumptions about the concept of motherhood, even the validity of "maternal instinct" as inherent and God-given, and to reconsider whether those qualities traditionally called "feminine" and "masculine" may not be artifacts of culture and not biologically determined after all.

There have always been women who found child rearing burdensome, motherhood ungratifying. (Throughout the ages rich women could with good conscience hire substitute mothers to suckle their infants and bring up their children. Indeed, these practices were taken for granted.) But to question openly the sanctity of motherhood was a profanity beside which whoredom seemed a virtue.

Today, in a society in which personal gratification often seems to take precedence over social responsibility and prerogatives over obligations; where the search for "personal fulfillment" becomes an end in itself, overriding social or moral considerations, it is hardly surprising that some women, dissatisfied, restless, discontented, pounce on the institution of marriage, with its obligatory compromises and restrictions on strictly personal desires, as the culprit responsible for their unhappiness. They feel boxed-in by their role of wife and mother, enslaved by husband and children, and envious of men's privileges to pursue ambitions, gratify desires, stride about freely in the big wide world without let or hindrance.

"Me too," the liberated mother cries as, like Ibsen's Nora, she walks out the door.

Reasons given for leaving differ. "Raising kids just isn't my bag," proclaims a vociferous women's libber as she leaves her offspring to her husband in the divorce agreement in order to be free to work in the movement.

Another wants "a life for myself" as she packs her bags to go off on an archaeological dig with her lover. "I did my job for fourteen years," Cissy W. cries. "I looked after a husband, three kids, two dogs, a cat, dozens of hamsters, a parakeet, a house, and a father-in-law. Now I want something for myself."

Still another leaves to "find her identity." "When I was a girl, I was Daddy's angel!" says Ida Mae D., as she tries to explain why she is leaving husband and children. "When I got married, I was Carter's wife. Then I was Junior's mamma. I don't know who I am. *I want to find myself.*"

In those situations in which the mother willingly relinquishes custody of the children to the father, his problems with the children are not unlike those of the separated or divorced mother (though hers are often more heavily burdened by financial strain). There are the unfamiliar demands of a domestic order; getting the children to help with chores; most important, finding enough time to be with them. And the necessity of explaining to friends, colleagues, and relatives what's going on and of trying to put a good face on it.

Always there is the problem of helping the children understand what's happened without their being devastated by their mother's seeming rejection of them. Children are bound to be puzzled and confused by this reversal of traditional sex roles. Such arrangements are still uncommon. The separating or divorcing mother who voluntarily leaves the household and children to the care of the father is still looked upon by the community, if not with the same disapproval or revulsion accorded the abandoning mother, at the very least as "some kind of nut"—an "unnatural" mother.

Whatever sense of loss the children may feel at the

mother's departure is compounded by their sensitivity to the attitudes of relatives, neighbors, and friends toward this atypical arrangement. To ask children to bear the brunt of the community's reaction to their parents' unconventional behavior or to their espousal of "radical" causes (unless the family happens to be living in a like-minded community) is to place a heavy burden on them.

For those children who have already been exposed to parental battles, to the kind of intolerable marital discord that finally led to the decision to separate, and to the frightening reality of a disrupted family, the extra blow of Mother's walking out can be very painful indeed. They will need extra help to accept and adjust to the new and strange circumstances. In one instance, the arrangement was presented so as to take on the aspect of a status symbol. The children were able to boast to their friends at school (a private progressive school, we might add, in which half the children were from separated or divorced families) that their mother had gone off to Harvard to get a doctoral degree!

Fortunately, in these unusual situations the children are spared some of the flak from the customary haggling over custody, alimony, and child support of more conventional divorce proceedings. Moreover, since such arrangements generally take place with the father's (if sometimes less than gleeful) consent, there seems to be less acrimony or vindictiveness than in more common separation or divorce situations.

Such a father is in a much better position to prepare his children for the radical change in their lives than is the father whose wife has eloped. As in the breaking-up period before the father actually leaves home, both parents have the opportunity to talk about the mother's impending departure with the children, to encourage their questions and the expression of their feelings, and to mitigate insofar as possible the trauma of seeing the family unit dissolved.

As when Father leaves, arrangements for regular visiting with the mother, inspection of her place of residence and work, can be made in advance of the separation. Having in their possession her telephone number and address can give the children at least a modicum of assurance that they can reach Mother whenever they wish and that she still loves and cherishes them despite her physical absence.

Split Custody: One for You, One for Me

It is not uncommon for divorcing parents to split the custody of the children between them, the older boys going with Dad, the girls and younger children with Mom. The theory underlying this arrangement is that growing boys need their fathers as model, companion, and guide for their optimal development, whereas girls and little children are better off with their mothers. While such a theory sounds eminently reasonable, its feasibility depends entirely upon the particular child and the particular situation. Applying rule-of-thumb principles doesn't necessarily work out. The child's best interests, in which age and sex are two elements, must always be the uppermost consideration.

We have found that in general the early adolescent boy's going with his father—assuming that *he wants to* and Father can arrange it—works out pretty well. Keep in mind that a family ruptured by divorce has been an unhappy, tormented family and that the children as well as the parents have been miserable, often for a very long time. Many a young adolescent in such a spot longs—indeed needs—to break away from home ties. This wish can be answered in gradual stages by his leaving the original family household, yet remaining under the protection of a responsible adult—in this case his own father. In addition, there is the relief to a growing boy of being spared the almost inevitable emotional pull of a husbandless mother and the guilt and turbulence of his own confused feelings toward her.

But split custody is no easy road for parent or child. Being parceled out is hard on children, no matter how considerate of their needs the arrangement may be. Jealousies and rivalries among the children living with different parents tend to be sharper, the chance of resentment against the custodial parent more likely.

Let us look at one such family:

After fifteen years of a stormy marriage, Ken and Adele S. were separated. Of their three children—Lenny, thirteen, Aaron, ten, and Melinda, eight—Lenny left the family home with the father one rainy night at 2 A.M. after a fifteen-round bout—a draw—between Ken and Adele.

Following are some excerpts from an interview with Ken.

INTERVIEWER: What happened the night you left?

KEN: We'd been fighting like cats and dogs half the night. I thought about breaking up many times, but it was hard to leave the children. But that night I decided that I'd had it up to here. I woke up Lenny, told him to get dressed, and we left.

INTERVIEWER: Had you prepared Lenny for the move?

KEN: It wasn't necessary. We never talked about it. But he knew that when I left, he would too. He and his mother never got along. She's a nervous Nellie, a worrywart, excitable, fussy—a perfectionist. Lenny's like me, slow, easygoing, sloppy. Most of our fights in the last couple of years were about him. She was always complaining about Lenny. I'd come home from work and the first thing out of her mouth was "Lenny did this," "Lenny did that." I'd be tired and hungry and before you knew it I'd be yelling and hollering at him for tormenting his mother. I'd get so worked up I couldn't eat. Later, long after I left, it came to me that what she complained about in Lenny was what was eating her about me but couldn't say. She was taking out her anger at me on him. I was drinking in those days, not enough to keep me from doing my job, but enough to make me ornery as hell at home.

Lenny and his father went to a hotel that night. The next day Ken found a small apartment in the neighborhood of Lenny's school so his son could continue there until graduation.

INTERVIEWER: How did the other children take this?

KEN: Aaron was jealous. He kept asking me, "Why can't I come too?" Imagine, three years after the separation he still keeps asking me. He must be having a rough time with his mother.

INTERVIEWER: Did Lenny visit his family after you left?

KEN: At first he didn't want to see his mother, but I insisted that he should go. Now he's over there a couple of times a week. Mind you, he can't just drop in; he has to telephone to get permission. You know, I think he and his mother really love each other even though they fight over everything. I believe he enjoys fighting with her. After all, he doesn't *have* to hang around that house! He can see Aaron and Melly at our place—they visit us every weekend.

Ken added that he also spends Wednesday afternoons with the boys as umpire for their Little League practice games and takes them out to dinner afterward.

INTERVIEWER: How did Lenny get along with you after the two of you were living alone?

KEN: Funny thing. When we lived home, even though I'd yell at him, we were like two buddies in a foxhole trying to dodge the bullets zooming by. At the beginning, after we got settled in our own place—you know, fixing it up and everything—things were great. We were like pals. Then he began falling down in his schoolwork and acting up with me. He'd argue about the least thing, complain this and that wasn't right; he wouldn't do his chores around the house; he'd fight with Aaron when the kids came for the weekend. He became a real pain in the ass.

INTERVIEWER: You and Lenny seem to be getting along fine now. How did you manage that?

KEN: It took quite a while. I was so involved with my own troubles—Adele kept raising the ante, especially after she learned about Fern—that I didn't give the boy as much attention as he needed. I guess the only way Lenny knew how to get it was to make trouble. The school counselor made me aware of that when I was called to see him because they were about to kick Lenny out of school. After the alimony, child support, and property settlement got squared away and I knew that Fern and I would finally be able to get married, I simmered down and so did he.

After two years of haggling over financial arrangements, Ken and Adele were finally divorced. Immediately after the divorce Ken married Fern, a young woman with a two-year-old boy from a previous marriage, whom he had met about six months after the separation and had introduced to the children a year later when he was certain she would become his second wife.

INTERVIEWER: How did Lenny react to Fern's coming into your life?

KEN: I was afraid Lenny would be jealous of her, but this didn't happen. They get along great—they're real pals. Fern is an unusually perceptive, understanding, and very pretty young woman who intuitively knows how to handle Lenny.

INTERVIEWER: How do Aaron and Melinda get along with Fern?

KEN: They love her. And she likes to have them here. You know about the new baby. When we get a larger apartment, we hope the kids will stay weekends with us.

Divided Custody

Still another form of custody is that in which the child spends a specified amount of time, commonly six months of the year, with each parent. Such an arrangement is generally made when the parents live a great distance apart, making visits by the noncustodial parent (usually the father) a practical impossibility. Whatever the reasons for such an arrangement, the child's best interests are seldom taken into consideration in making it, for it works a great hardship on a child. We know one eight-year-old girl who, as a solution to the fierce custody battle waged over her, spends one week with one parent, the next week with the other! (The parents live in the same school district, so she attends one school.) Clearly, this arrangement has more to do with the parents' need to keep their own fighting relationship going than with the child's best interests. Putting a good face on it, the child says she likes the arrangement, because now she has two of everything. But her disturbed hehavior and her emotional distress hint otherwise.

Divided custody generally means disrupting the child's surroundings, his schooling, his social activities, his friendships. Perhaps the most deleterious aspect of divided custody is that it disturbs the continuity of the relationship with either parent. While an older child can manage this, both because he grows less dependent upon his parents and because his parents are by now such an integral part of him, for the young child this continuity is essential for his emotional development.

A better arrangement—though far from ideal and still divided custody—would be to allow the child to spend the school year with one parent and the vacation period with the other. While this tends to limit the noncustodial parental relationship to that of "vacation" father or mother, it is less disruptive to the child's life.

Boarding School

Sometimes the fighting between the embattled parents rages so fiercely or the divorce situation in other respects is so adverse to the child's physical or mental health that it is in his best interests to remove him from the aegis of either parent. If no relatives or other persons are available to care for him properly, boarding school, if it can be afforded, may be the best solution until matters are resolved.

Boarding schools for the most part are neither Dick Stover's halcyon days nor George Orwell's hell hole. A boarding school can be a temporary haven for a child torn asunder by contending parents, a sanctuary from the parental fray. There, the unhappy child will find other children of separation or divorce with whom he can not only share companionship but find comfort in seeing that others are in the same boat. If he is lucky, he may also find an understanding teacher or other adult who will serve him as an ego ideal, someone whom he can admire and try to emulate. Indeed, the experience of being away from home at a good boarding school can give him a sense of belonging.

The trouble with sending a child off to boarding school at so crucial a time as the breakup of the family is that he very likely may feel his parents want to get rid of him (it may be true) and that he may well react with emotional disturbances or behavior problems. Assuming that it is not true that you want to get rid of him, but that you are taking this step to spare him exposure to constant turmoil, you will have to help him understand why going away to school is best for him at this time. Take him to visit the school and if possible to talk with a student who has attended it. Of course, you will keep in touch with him by mail and visits. It is surprising how adaptable most children can be to painful life situations about which they have no choice and how they somehow manage to find pleasure in the very things they gripe about to you.

Whatever the physical arrangements for the child's care may be, they are of secondary significance to the relationship between parent and child. Even though the father may see his child rarely, steady communication between the two can hold the relationship steadfast. It can keep bright the image of the father in the heart of the child.

12
ADOLESCENCE

Most children who live full-time with the separated or divorced father are going through the stage of development known as adolescence, a period that covers the age span from twelve through nineteen. Actually this period includes several different and distinct, though overlapping, stages—puberty (roughly, twelve to fourteen), when physical changes are paramount, and social, emotional, and intellectual changes begin to appear; early adolescence (roughly, fourteen to sixteen); and late adolescence (roughly, sixteen to nineteen)—each with its own characteristics. The manifestations of each stage differ for each child and appear at different times for each child, depending on the rate of development of his physical, intellectual, emotional, and social growth, each of which proceeds at its own pace. For example, a fourteen-year-old child may have reached the physical development of a sixteen-year-old but the emotional development of a twelve-year-old.

Adolescents can be a joy. They can also drive you mad. Let's listen in on two fathers discussing their adolescent sons over lunch.

Sam is telling Henry about the problems he's having with his twelve-year-old Clint. How he talks back to his mother, fights with his sister, doesn't come home in time for dinner.

"When I question him or bawl him out, he just gets sullen and clams up. He used to be a regular chatterbox. Now if you ask him anything, he just grunts 'Yeah' or 'Nah.' And dirty! Marge always had a hard time getting him to wash or take a bath, but he'd do it. Now, if you tell him he can't sit down at the table with dirty hands, he stalks off to his room in a huff. And his room! A regular pigpen, dirty clothes lying around, collections of junk he won't let anyone touch. She thinks he's smoking—found a half-empty pack of cigarettes in his drawer when she went to put away his laundry. When Marge asked him about it, he said he was holding it for one of his pals. He never used to lie. I don't know what's eating the kid."

Henry replies, "You think you've got problems? Wait till Clint hits sixteen, like my Hank. Or even fourteen. I tell you, the bigger the kid gets, the more problems you have. You remember what a smart little kid Hank was when he was six? Followed me around like Mary's lamb. You remember that time I brought him down to the office and he said he was going to be a 'turney' like his Dad when he grew up? Attorney! I'll be lucky if he makes it through high school. He keeps threatening to drop out of school and hitchhike out West with his friend Corky, another character. Believe me, he won't have to drop out; the school will drop him out, his grades are so low. In grammar school he was top of his class. A great little pitcher, too, with the Little League. And he was a swimming champ at camp. I tell you, no father could have been prouder of any kid.

"Well, you should see him now. Looks like some overgrown freak. Long stringy hair hanging over his eyes, ugly fuzz on his face to hide the pimples, his nose and lips sort of swollen looking. His clothes look like they came out of a ragbag. The kids he hangs around with are just as miserable as he. They sit around in the den like a bunch of zombies, drinking beer and not saying a word. Or they're blasting their damn rock 'n' roll records loud enough to bust your eardrums. You're worrying about cigarettes? I'm sure Hank and his pals smoke pot when they lock themselves in his room. Clare claims there's a mighty funny smell when she goes in there to clean up.

"Talk about arguing! You should hear Hank. He argues about every single damn thing, from who should take out the garbage to Mao Tse-tung. And he contradicts everything either of us say even before he hears us out. According to Hank we're a couple of reactionary dodoes who don't know the score about anything. He fights with everybody at home, his sisters, his brother. Yet, you know, that nut, on Mother's Day he bought Clare a bouquet of flowers must have cost him his week's allowance. And when he's in a good mood, there couldn't be a better kid—the old Hank. The other day he fixed Jody's bike; he drove Becky to a school party and fetched her home later. He mowed the lawn without even being asked, and last Sunday he helped me build a patio—enjoyed doing it, too. Funny. Just when you're ready to give up on him, he turns into the old loving, helpful, considerate Hank. I just can't make out this generation."

Sam and Henry are not separated or divorced fathers discussing two disturbed adolescents. They are two married men going through the usual trials of raising two normal boys during that rocky stage between childhood and manhood called adolescence.

Adolescence—A Disturbing Phase to Parents

Each stage in a child's development evokes a special response in a parent. Some parents find one stage more trying (or more pleasurable) than another. When it comes to adolescence, practically all parents find it disturbing. All of a sudden your young son or daughter is transformed into a man or woman. In actual fact, however, there is nothing precipitous about adolescence. It is a gradual developmental stage on a continuum from childhood to adulthood, during which certain crucial life tasks must be mastered if the boy or girl is eventually to become an emotionally healthy, well-functioning, productive adult.

What are these tasks? One is to achieve *sexual maturity.* Another is to separate oneself from the original family, to find one's own identity and *establish oneself as an independent adult.*

The adolescent's changes can bring to mind, sometimes painfully, our own adolescence. In our son's defiance, in his criticism of us, we are reminded of our harsh judgment of our own parents when we were his age. We may not have been as outspoken as today's youth—in these days our children are expected to speak their mind—but we criticized our parents, if only in our thoughts and fantasies, just as passionately. When we become the targets of our son's criticism, we may react excessively without realizing why, and we may rebuke or punish him for our own youthful defiant or hostile feelings.

Of all the characteristics of adolescence, the young person's physical changes, his emergent sexual maturity, may be the most unsettling to parents. The bodily changes that excite, or alarm, the pubertal child may also excite, or alarm, the parent. Whether or not we admit it, the presence in the house of a blooming boy or girl is sexually stimulating. The young person's omnipresent preoccupation with sex is bound to be disquieting. Erotic "emanations" can reactivate the parent's own adolescent struggles with sex and stir up conflicting feelings in the present that cannot be brushed under the rug. They may trigger off old repressed feelings that can blind the parent in dealing with the young person in a rational way.

Fathers react to the sexual maturity of their adolescent sons in many ways. Most fathers take pride in their sons' emerging manhood. In some cultures the father initiates the boy into the mysteries of the sex act by enlisting the ministrations of a prostitute or older woman. (French literature is replete with stories of upper-class mothers requesting their women friends to initiate their sons into the art of love.)

While this practice is uncommon among American families, some fathers tacitly encourage a boy's sexual exploits, perhaps for their own vicarious satisfaction, by sexual innuendoes, telling "dirty stories," and even eliciting and exchanging confidences. (These selfsame fathers might rail against any evidence of sexual activity in their daughters.)

Other fathers—perhaps to clamp down upon their own vagrant erotic fantasies—frown upon their sons' sexual ventures and hammer away at the dangers of venereal disease, forced marriage, and child support. We have known fathers who picked on their sons for poor schoolwork, lack of ambition, and laziness—all of them justifiable complaints, but which at bottom proved to be rationalizations for their envy of their sons' sexual ascendancy. A mature father, whatever his feelings about his own sexual prowess, takes pride in his son's waxing sexual powers, accepting them not only as part of the natural evolution of man's life cycle but as an affirmation of his own immortality.

Father's Reaction to the Adolescent Girl's Sexual Maturity

Adolescent girls put greater emphasis than boys do on their burgeoning secondary sex characteristics—the developing breasts, rounding hips, axillary and pubic hair—since these are to them the most blatant symbols of being grown up. From wearing provocative clothes and makeup and running around with boys to sexual promiscuity, the adolescent girl uses her sexuality as an instrument of defiance against parental authority and as a declaration of her independence.

The relationship of a father to his young daughter as she arrives at early adolescence takes a special turn. Many fathers tell us that the metamorphosis of a daughter from a little girl to a young woman creeps up on them unawares. Suddenly, or so it seems, she emerges dramatically like a butterfly from the cocoon of her childhood. One day she's a gawky, sexless kid, all skinny legs and arms. The next day she's a soft round plum, a mysterious creature, half inviting, half shy, exuding some vague erotic aura of which she pretends to be unaware.

Adolescence, announced so dramatically by puberty, is a stage in the developmental process from infancy to adulthood. Like every stage of development, it does not progress in a straight line. Until the new stage is consolidated, there is bound to be a temporary return now and then, generally in a crisis situation, to an earlier and more comfortable stage. We've seen our thirteen-year-old, decked out in a long gown, padded bra, and false eyelashes, waiting for her date to escort her to her first dance. The next day she's back to playing jump rope.

Most fathers take pride in their daughters' femininity. They enjoy their teasing and flirtatiousness—all girls who have a good relationship with their fathers practice their feminine arts on Daddy. A father reported with great amusement how his eleven-year-old appeared in the living room one evening in her underwear to "show Daddy my first bra."

Comes a time, however, when father and daughter begin to feel self-conscious about her sitting on his lap, roughing up his hair, or wrestling around in horseplay; when they feel uncomfortable about physical contact; when the warning is writ large: DO NOT TOUCH!

Fathers react in different ways to their daughters' transformation into womanhood. Some fathers become anxious over their awareness of their daughters' sexuality, and to quell their anxiety they behave in a cross or even cruel way. A father came to a therapy session overwhelmed with guilt and shame. The previous night his fifteen-year-old daughter, a fully developed beautiful youngster, came home after midnight looking rather disheveled and excited. The sight of her body, provocatively outlined by her sweater and skintight jeans, so inflamed the father that he found himself yelling at her and calling her vile names. Other fathers deny the evidence of their daughters' sexual maturity and continue to regard them as their "little girls" practically up to the moment they become mothers.

Separation or divorce at the time of a daughter's adolescence presents special problems. The father generally sees his daughter at prescribed intervals and often in a contrived and impersonal setting, such as a restaurant or hotel lobby. Moreover, the adolescent girl, meeting her father on a "date," may dress or behave in a more seductive manner than if she saw him at home every day. The impact of her femaleness under these circumstances makes some fathers uncomfortable.

On the other hand, one divorced father we know, in his late forties, quite vain over his youthful appearance, takes pleasure in imagining that people mistake his eighteen-year-old daughter for his girl friend and envy him. He wines and dines her in fashionable restaurants and pays her attentive court when they are out together. "I bet those people at the next table are thinking, 'What's that old geezer doing with that young chick?'" he will whisper in her ear. While this half amuses her, she feels uncomfortable about that kind of play-acting, for it arouses her childhood wishes—and fears—about having Father all to herself.

Struggle for Independence

Perhaps the next most striking feature of adolescence is the young person's need to free himself from his dependence on his parents—to find his identity and eventually establish himself as an adult. In his march toward independence—two steps forward, one step back—he fights against parental restrictions, whether they be over the length of his hair, the hours he keeps, or the use of the family car. What parents call back talk he regards as his Declaration of Independence. The arguments go on—and on. Necessary parental or other controls over his behavior—at this age his judgment is often none too good—he considers an invasion of his private rights, and he fights fiercely against the injustices of his tyrannical parents and society.

In his struggle, he must devalue his parents—their ideas, their values, their way of life. He has an uncanny ability to ferret out your weaknesses, expose flaws in your arguments, spot contradictions in your logic, define you once and for all as stupid, unfeeling, and unworthy of his childhood admiration and love.

He is even more maddening. While you are brooding about his disobedience, his callous disregard for your feelings, or are wracked with doubt over your refusal of a preposterous request (followed by his stalking out), he shows up a few hours later a loving, dependent child, asking, "What's for supper?" This return to the security of his role as a child reminds one of a two-year-old who scampers away from his mother to explore the world, then runs back to the safety of her lap.

The need for the security of home and family, especially at critical times, is particularly true of the pre- and early adolescent, though it is characteristic of all young people. Some deny this need by actually taking off for faraway places or leaving home for long periods or for good. But the nostalgia for home, even the most miserable, wells up in everyone, especially in time of illness or trouble. Robert Frost defined home as "the place where, when you have to go there/ They have to take you in." Adolescents need that comforting thought. Though they may rail against family ties, those ties "shut out loneliness," as one eighteen-year-old, far away from home, put it.

Who Am I?

In the adolescent's struggle against authority figures, a few special adults manage to escape the tarred brush of scorn he or she so freely applies to the older generation. These persons may be some public personality, such as a political leader, an athlete, or an entertainer, or someone within his or her immediate circle like a teacher or coach or even pal Freddy's father—the selfsame father, one might add, whom Freddy is downgrading. These demigods are endowed with qualities the adolescent admires and even tries to emulate. They serve a useful purpose in his development. Through his identification with them, he can delineate for himself a variety of ideas, values, and philosophies of life that in the long run help define him as a person.

Who am I? is a question that preoccupies the adolescent. Identifying with an admired father figure moves him a step closer to an answer. More important, perhaps, he can transfer onto these figures those warm, positive feelings toward his father that he must now repudiate—only temporarily, it is to be hoped—in his struggle toward independence. A thirteen-year-old boy we know, who is fiercely critical of his divorced father, adores his father's twin brother, on whom the boy bestows his highest accolade: "Uncle Ted's okay."

Peer Group

The adolescent's main pillar of support during the transitional period between childhood and adulthood is his peer group. The opinions of his friends far outweigh anything his parents may say. Their pronouncements are holy writ. At the same time that he fights against the authority of his parents, teachers, and the community, and fancies himself a rebel against the Establishment, the authority of his peer group is unquestioned. With the scrupulosity of a zealot, he conforms to its dictates on every matter—clothes, hair style, food, music, language, art, even ideas. Especially ideas. The structure of the peer society gives him that security he so desperately needs while he is trying on the various guises of adulthood.

Along the way he generally has a best friend—in early adolescence he is usually of the same sex—with whom he shares his confidences, his dreams, his ambitions. Once he "falls in love," however, the influence of his peer group and even of his best friend dwindles, in part because he wants to spend all his time with the beloved, in part because they have served their purpose. And eventually, like the toddler who one day turns into a small boy, the boy becomes a man. Until then you will have to tolerate the brushing aside of all you hold dear with his irrefutable rebuttal "But my friend Gary says—," or even the more hurtful "But Gary's father says—."

Mood Swings

We are all familiar with, and often baffled by, the mood swings of the adolescent. If we dare recall our own adolescence, with its ecstasies one moment and its miseries the next, its excitement today and its boredom tomorrow, its joys of comradeship and its agonizing loneliness, we thank heaven it's over.

Some of the wide and occasionally sudden variations in mood are due to physiological processes—increased endocrine and other biological activity that influences feelings. But by no means all are due to physiology. Adolescence is a time of endless fantasies, a time of soaring hopes and abysmal fears. The anticipation—and dread—of leaving childhood for unknown adventures in the big wide world; the challenges of approaching manhood or womanhood with its joys and sorrows of love and sex; the pressures, both from within himself and from his environment, to choose a vocation and a way of life, which means forsaking other equally desirable though contradictory choices—all contribute to the mood swings of the adolescent.

His mood swings, both high and low, are universal. He can feel rambunctious and ebullient. He can also feel sad and alone, hopeless and unworthy, unloved and unlovable. He feels ashamed as well as excited by his fantasies of violence against those close to him and of rampant sex in all its infinite variety. And when sometimes he acts out these fantasies by torturing an animal or engaging in sex play with sister or pal, afterward the young adolescent is tormented by guilt and feelings of self-loathing. As one fourteen-year-old put it, "Sometimes I feel lower than whale shit."

Whether depression is more frequent among children of divorce, we do not know. We do know it is a common symptom of adolescence. For children of divorce, the usual conflicts of adolescence are compounded not only by their own conflicts of loyalty to one parent or another, but by the opposing tugs of each parent and by their own ambivalent feelings to which they may respond with apathy or depression.

Exceptions that Prove the Rule

While the foregoing course of development is typical of adolescents in general, it is by no means universal. Some youngsters are so alarmed by the bodily changes and strange feelings that pervade them that they inhibit insofar as possible their sexuality. Some, like the loner, hang back from the challenges that a peer group presents. Some youngsters, whether through timidity or fear or a need to be pleasing to adults, may show no sign of rebelliousness toward parents or community. They are generally regarded as "good" children because they don't talk back or make trouble. We know, however, that their mixed-up love-hate feelings toward those they need must be hiding somewhere. Sometimes these feelings are expressed in physical symptoms or in hostile thoughts or in depression. Sometimes in fantasies and daydreaming. Sometimes in music, art, or poetry. Sometimes in religion.

There are other children who gallop wildly into adolescence. These children are generally endowed with a superabundance of energy and drive. Because of some great inner push toward growing up or a push from the environment—and often both—they can't wait to take on the trappings of a man or woman. Because these children are frequently restless, hyperactive, impulsive youngsters whose judgment lags behind the development of their bodies, they are pushovers for getting into trouble. Many delinquents fall into this category.

Most children, even the laggards and the gallopers, manage to make it through adolescence to adulthood without too great a cost. For those who get mired along the way, professional help may be necessary.

13
LIVING WITH THE ADOLESCENT

In the inevitable war between the opposing parents to hold or capture their children's loyalty, the father whose adolescent child voluntarily comes to live with him, whether at the time of the divorce as the child's custodial choice or at some later time, is bound to feel a sense of victory: Aha! Judy (or Jimmie) prefers *me* to *her!*

Without for a moment questioning the sincerity of your child's love or preference for you at the time, it is well to be prepared that he may change his mind later. Children of separation or divorce seem to be especially vulnerable to the ups and downs of adolescence. It may be that the child's choice has as much to do with his intense feelings toward his mother—be they loving or hating—as with his desire to throw in his lot with you.

This doesn't mean that your son's decision to live with you is not a good choice. It may relieve him of the hazards inherent in living alone with his mother—especially those incestuous fantasies, incited by the pervasiveness and urgency of his sexual drives during this period of development, that can be so very disturbing to the adolescent boy. Feelings of self-hatred at this time of life are common. Often the boy behaves badly toward the mother, as though to deny to himself his loathsome and frightening thoughts. Moreover, the mother may unwittingly turn to the boy for emotional support, burden him with unwanted confidences or complaints against the absent father, and refer to the son, and indeed even regard him, as an ersatz "man of the house," compounding his feelings of guilt even further.

It is not unusual, therefore, that during adolescence the boy turns to his father for protection against these disturbing feelings. His excuses for leaving Mother are legion: "She tries to keep me a baby. She won't let me play football; she's afraid I'll get hurt." "She keeps picking on me all the time. You know what a nag she is."

An adolescent girl, in her need to free herself from her ambivalent ties to her mother, begs Dad to let her come live with him. "Mom criticizes everything I say or do. She's impossible to live with." Father is overjoyed. At last he is vindicated. His son or daughter understands now why he couldn't get along with their mother; why he had to get away from home.

But wait. There may be a hitch. If the youngster has shifted custody from one parent to another out of motives of spite or revenge—parent switching is a cruel weapon adolescents sometimes use to get back at the custodial parent for robbing them of an intact family—or if he has not worked out his feelings about the forsaken parent, the chances are that he may just as readily switch back or, out of guilt or confused feelings, unwittingly manage to stir up trouble. This is especially likely to happen if you are remarried or involved with a woman friend or otherwise fail to live up to the child's fantasies about what life with you will be like, fantasies that are bound to be unrealistic and sometimes even absurd. This is particularly true of the adolescent girl and her father.

The Divorced Father and the Adolescent Girl

Even in intact families and with the smoothest of mother-daughter relationships, the onset of puberty in the young girl tends to stir up undercurrents of rivalry toward the mother.

The separation or divorce situation intensifies them, brings them to the surface. No matter what the facts, the adolescent girl secretly believes that her mother was responsible for Father's leaving home and hence for Father's leaving *her*. She may deny such feelings to herself by being unduly close, unduly loving to Mother. But commonly she begins to complain, to argue, to make Mother's life miserable.

Mother, struggling to cope with the financial and social hardships imposed by her changed economic and social status, may well find her daughter's exasperating behavior beyond her patience or strength to handle alone and she may turn to the girl's father for help. Father (perhaps secretly believing he will succeed with his daughter where her mother failed) takes daughter to live with him and his new wife. His new wife isn't happy about it, but under the circumstances there seems nothing else to do. What happens?

Troublemaker

One would think that all the adolescent daughters who come to live with their fathers have read the same script, the basic elements of their stories are so similar . . .

Take the H. family. Lewis and Vera H. were divorced after fourteen years of marriage and three children: Bonnie, twelve; Alice, eight; and Eileen, six. Vera moved with the children to a town more than five hundred miles away to be close to her parents. Lewis, a university professor, visited the children every other weekend at considerable financial sacrifice, since these visits meant taking rooms at a motel so the children could stay with him for the weekend.

Bonnie, a buxom, rambunctious, already fully developed twelve-year-old, had always been a problem to her mother. Vera could never understand or handle her. "It was as though they came from two different planets," Lewis said.

Taking Bonnie away from her beloved father with whom

she used to have fun—skating and bicycling with him, helping him make repairs around the house—only added to her resentment against her cold, distant mother (Bonnie's description). Bonnie hated her new school and teachers, fought with her classmates, failed in her studies, sassed Grandma, took up with the lower elements in town. Lewis was constantly receiving long-distance calls from Vera complaining about Bonnie and asking him what to do. And Bonnie kept bugging him to take her back with him so that she could return to her old school, her old friends, her old house.

Finally when Bonnie was fourteen, after a particularly bad scene—she was caught smoking pot—Lewis consented to take her to live with him. "Bonnie couldn't have been better," he reported. "She cooked for me, kept the house clean, did well in school, had lots of friends. I really enjoyed having her around."

Lewis was seeing Norma, a young colleague in her late twenties, and Bonnie often joined them in their outings. "Bonnie adored Norma," Lewis reported. "Kept saying how pretty she was, how sweet, why didn't we get married? Well, Norma and I did get married, on Bonnie's fifteenth birthday, and the three of us had a big bash. Bonnie *seemed* to be as happy as Norma and I were."

It didn't take long, however, before a serious rivalry erupted between the two females. Norma's jealousy was covert, apparent only in her constant complaints: Bonnie was sloppy, uncooperative, dressed like a hippy, used vile language, to say nothing of her choice of friends. Bonnie's jealousy was obvious. A year after the marriage, when Norma became pregnant, Bonnie became pregnant too, the result of a casual encounter with a seventeen-year-old boy. She was aborted.

By this time Bonnie's relationship with her mother had deteriorated to such an extent that she could not return there. And, though she still "behaved like a little lamb" with her father, the bickering between her and Norma never stopped. Norma found her presence intolerable. Bonnie was sent to a boarding school, but she regarded this as punishment and behaved so outrageously that she had to be removed. She returned to live in her father's household in what she refers to as an "armed truce."

The Divorced Father and Conflict with the Adolescent Boy

Some conflict between parent and child at any age is inevitable. The child wants what he wants; the parent, as the transmitter of society's rules, must arbitrate between the child's self-centered wishes and the demands of society. The child resists. A clash follows.

In adolescence this clash rings loud. As the young person's intelligence expands, he begins to examine the social, moral, political, and religious beliefs of his parents and the society they represent, attitudes and actions that up to that time he had more or less taken for granted. He begins to criticize his parents for their little hypocrisies, point out inconsistencies between their words and their deeds. Verbal conflicts in this impersonal arena of ideas serve as a useful staging ground for the adolescent's more personal struggle to free himself emotionally from his parents. Most parents take their children's arguments and accusations in their stride, knowing from experience something the child has yet to learn—that one day he, too, will have to make those compromises between ideals and reality that now he can afford so virtuously to condemn.

To the divorced father, however, the young person's criticisms, which might be ignored or handled casually in the intact family setting, tend to loom large and assume significance beyond all proportion. The experience of divorce, with its traumatic underlayer of failure in a basic human relationship, tends to shake a man's confidence in his mandates about family matters. As one divorced father put it: "When I crack down on my son and he taunts me with 'Who are you to tell me what to do? I don't see that you've done such a great job with your life,' that's hitting me below the belt, and I feel like walloping him. But I can't help wondering if maybe he's right. How can I expect him to take my demands seriously when he sees what a mess I've made of my life?" So he backtracks and becomes conciliatory, or—and this is more likely—he reacts with defensive anger and even outrage. And his rightful place in the boy's life as a wise authority figure is undermined.

Dealing with the Adolescent

Adolescence is a tough time for parents as well as teen-agers. It is particulary tough in this period of history when social, cultural, and moral values are breaking down at a rapid rate; a period when parents themselves, throughout the ages the transmitters of the culture to the next generation, are confused. They can't help but sympathize with their adolescent's indignation at corruption in high places, his relentless questioning of traditions long held dear, even though they may disagree with his way of expressing his disdain and disillusionment.

"What can I do?" the bewildered father asks, confused and unhappy about the exasperating behavior of his teen-ager. "How can I help him grow up to become a responsible adult, yet not make him feel that I'm bossing him around? Do I have the right to interfere when I see him floundering around, not making any sense? Or must I stand aside and watch him ruin himself because he insists upon finding his own way in his own crazy, mixed-up fashion?" These are not easy questions to answer.

One thing to do is to ask yourself, in your calmer moments and out of the presence of the adolescent—it's almost impossible to be calm in his presence—What's he trying to tell me by his behavior?

You Are Not His Therapist

Trying to understand your child's behavior does not mean trying to "treat" him. You are the child's father, not his therapist. You are blessed and burdened with all the privileges and responsibilities of fatherhood. To talk things over with the adolescent, each hearing the other out, can help to clear the air when disagreements get out of hand. It can even strengthen the relationship. But telling him *why* he is behaving badly can only confuse and upset him. As one thirteen-year-old exploded, "One thing drives me nuts is when my mother makes like a shrink." Here he pitches his voice high and in a mocking, synthetically sweet tone, he mimics, " 'You hit Molly because you think I love her more than you. I love you both alike.' That's a lot of crap."

The Risks of Single Parenthood

Understanding does not mean tolerance of behavior that is hurtful to the adolescent or others—or to you. The adolescent may rear up and snort and kick, but if it is necessary to bridle him for his own protection and that of others, you must do so with the authority that is your responsibility as his parent and guardian. For all their rebelliousness, young people need—and want—limits, if only to try themselves out against them. Certainly, the young adolescent feels more secure if he knows *for sure* what he may and what he may not do, though he may experiment with the latter.

Even the older adolescent needs the authority and mature guidance of his father or some other older adult who can serve as an authority figure or counselor during this transitional period. Though the seventeen- or eighteen-year-old, already half-man, may assume all the trappings of adulthood, from beard and job to steady girl friend, he is still also half-boy.

Of course, the firmness must be tempered with affection. Kids know, no matter how much they grumble, when restrictions are imposed through genuine concern. They also know when they are a punitive ukase, imposed by a more powerful authoritarian figure out of a power struggle to show who's boss.

The separated or divorced father whose children live with him runs a greater risk of being overindulgent than if he were still living in an intact family. No matter how inevitable or imperative the separation or divorce, there is bound to be some residue of guilt toward the children for disrupting their family that may unconsciously propel the father to be overindulgent in an effort to make up to them. As one divorced father put it, "I know they con me into giving them things they don't need. And I let them do things I should say No to. But I don't want our time together to be a hassle."

Or a father may be too indulgent through overidentification with his offspring, giving to them what he himself may have wanted and been deprived of in his youth. A divorced father we know, yielding to the importunate wheedling of his seventeen-year-old son, an impulsive, reckless lad, gave him a motorcycle for his birthday, something the father had craved as a boy but that his family could not afford. He did so against his own better judgment and the wishes of the boy's mother and her new husband. The predictable happened. The boy and a companion were badly injured in an accident with the motorcycle within a week of receiving the gift.

The same father, grief stricken at having been indirectly instrumental in his son's injury, recognized still another irrational motive for the inappropriate gift—his jealousy of the stepfather and the need to prove to the boy a love greater than his rival's. In the divorce situation, the temptation to say Yes when the other parent says No is sometimes irresistible.

Know Thyself

It is always easier, and more comfortable, to try to understand someone else's behavior than your own. There comes a time, however, if you find yourself more disturbed, angry, or obsessed with your adolescent's behavior than is warranted, when you must ask yourself the question Why am I so upset?

It is not easy to think clearly—or to think at all, for that matter—when your eighteen-year-old Annabelle tells you she's moved in with her boy friend. Or when Cliff declares that college is just another tool of the capitalistic system: he's not going back to school; he's joining a commune in Maine where they'll grow their own potatoes and make their own shoes. It would be peculiar, indeed, if you did not react with some vehemence to what you consider self-destructive or irresponsible or downright idiotic behavior. And it is your responsibility as a caring parent and as a wiser, more experienced person to tell your adolescents what you think and how you feel. (This doesn't mean they will follow your counsel. Or that they necessarily should. But that's another matter.)

Ruminating about what has so unnerved you, you may find that your child's action had touched off some experience of your youth, or even some half-buried fantasy you would have best left forgotten. Like his maturing sexuality, the adolescent's struggle to separate himself from his family can have a most unsettling effect upon a parent. A father told us how he "hit the roof" when his eighteen-year-old son, admitted to Harvard, told him he was not entering college in the fall. Instead, he was signing on with a tuna-fishing boat going to South America as soon as he could obtain the necessary union papers. He thought he should see a "slice of real life before settling down," he asserted. One might have expected this father to have been sympathetic to his son's decision, since he himself had run away from home around the same age.

Although the circumstances surrounding his departure were quite different—he had left after a brutal physical fight with his father—his son's announcement stirred up all the pain and chaos and guilt he had experienced during that disorganized, anarchic period of his life. In the two years he had bummed around the country, during which he served a brief jail sentence for vagrancy and spent several weeks in a hospital for a fractured skull sustained in a brawl, his father had died suddenly and his mother had been committed to a mental hospital. All through the years he had felt unaccountably guilty for his father's death and was consumed with regret that he had not been home to make peace with him before he died. When his son declared his intention to leave home, a storm of conflicting emotions overwhelmed him.

Admittedly, this is a rather extreme example, but it highlights the irrational feelings that can be aroused when your assertive adolescent, whom you continue to regard as a mere child, takes the reins of his life into his own hands. Moreover, even as you are taking pride in the bright promise of your offspring, a note of regret is bound to creep in at the inevitable distancing between you. We are all familiar with parents who continue to support their adult children well beyond the point where they could be self-supporting as a last-ditch maneuver to hold onto the child and postpone as long as possible his evolution as a full-fledged adult apart from the family.

All this applies to the parent-adolescent relationship in any family, intact or broken. But the strain is bound to be greater on the separated or divorced father. Deviations from expected behavior tend to be magnified and the father's reactions more aggravated than if he were living with the adolescent in a two-parent family situation.

In the long run, perhaps the prime requisite of dealing with an adolescent is a sense of humor. A sense of humor and a feeling of empathy. Remember your own adolescence with its often comic, sometimes heroic, sometimes pathetic, occasionally awesome, aspects. Remember when all adults, save for a favored few, were automatically viewed with suspicion and doubt. It's only justice that now it's your turn to be IT.

When Professional Help May Be Needed

Lest we be too sanguine, however, that the paradoxes of adolescence will eventually resolve themselves in the course of time, some behavior may betoken pathology that requires professional help. It is not always easy to know when some of the "crazy" things an adolescent does—like "dropping out," experimenting with drugs, or trying a new religion—are passing manifestations of the adolescent's efforts to "find himself"—to find out who he is and what he wants to do with his life—and when they spell some pathological disorganization of his self that requires professional help. You must try to recognize also when the relationship between parent and adolescent has so deteriorated that professional intervention is needed to help resolve the impasse.

In general, however, parents can take comfort in the knowledge that "time will darken it." Most parents and their adolescent children manage to survive those turbulent years without murdering each other. Indeed, they usually go on to a quite manageable and sometimes even congenial relationship. As the youngsters grow up, marry, and have children of their own, they discover, sometimes to their surprise, that their parents were neither as stupid nor as benighted as they had once considered them. They may even find that they share common interests and ideas and that their philosophies of life are not so far apart.

With luck, your grown-up children may even begin to enjoy your company. About this time, it may be solacing to know, *they* will start having trouble with their own children. And come to you for counsel.

EPILOGUE

Saturday afternoon at McDonald's. There's no mistaking them, part-time father and child on their weekly visit together, eating their hamburgers and sipping their chocolate milk shakes. You can spot the freshly bereaved pair—the child silent or sullen or red-eyed; the father tense, anxious, unhappy. Over there is a pair not so recently separated, but not yet settled in their still-strange roles, performing their visitation rites—the child restless, squirmy, eyes darting randomly around the impersonal restaurant as though seeking succor from the indifferent patrons; the father equally uncomfortable or bored or trying overhard to please, pressing still another hamburger on his resistant child. In the corner is a relaxed, friendly pair enjoying each other's company, chatting together easily, each clearly interested in what the other has to say. After much travail, having crossed a seemingly endless gap, this father and child have finally made it.